ALL THE THINGS
THEY SAID WE
COULDN'T HAVE

of related interest

Transitions
Our Stories of Being Trans
Foreword by Sabah Choudrey, Juno Roche and Meg-John Barker
ISBN 978 1 78775 851 3
eISBN 978 1 78775 852 0

Trans Power
Own Your Gender
Juno Roche
ISBN 978 1 78775 019 7
eISBN 978 1 78775 020 3

Supporting Trans People of Colour
How to Make Your Practice Inclusive
Sabah Choudrey
ISBN 978 1 78775 059 3
eISBN 978 1 78775 060 9

Yes, You Are Trans Enough
My Transition from Self-Loathing to Self-Love
Mia Violet
ISBN 978 1 78592 315 9
eISBN 978 1 78450 628 5

All The Things They Said We Couldn't Have

Stories of Trans Joy

T. C. Oakes-Monger

Illustrated by Flatboy

Jessica Kingsley Publishers
London and Philadelphia

First published in Great Britain in 2023 by Jessica Kingsley Publishers
An imprint of Hodder & Stoughton Ltd
An Hachette Company

1

Disclaimer: The information contained in this book is not intended
to replace the services of trained medical professionals or to be a
substitute for medical advice. You are advised to consult a doctor
on any matters relating to your health, and in particular on any
matters that may require diagnosis or medical attention.

A CIP catalogue record for this title is available from
the British Library and the Library of Congress

ISBN 978 1 83997 149 5
eISBN 978 1 83997 150 1

Printed and bound in Great Britain by TJ Books Limited

Jessica Kingsley Publishers' policy is to use papers that are natural,
renewable and recyclable products and made from wood grown in
sustainable forests. The logging and manufacturing processes are expected
to conform to the environmental regulations of the country of origin.

Jessica Kingsley Publishers
Carmelite House
50 Victoria Embankment
London EC4Y 0DZ

www.jkp.com

For every trans person who has been told that joy is something you cannot have.

For everyone whose stories are in this book and everyone who brings joy into my life.

For you reading this, because you bought a book about trans joy, and that is power.

For Noonie, you bring the brightest joy to my days. Dw i'n caru ti, am byth.

And finally, for me. For 15-year-old and 18-year-old and 21-year-old me, who didn't know that so much joy was on its way but fought to stick around anyway.

Contents

Author's Note

In this book I write about the experiences from my life. Our community is not a monolith, and I could never speak for us all. The experiences of trans people of colour occur at the intersections of racism and trans-phobia and result in unique forms of oppression. Classism, ableism and other forms of discrimination impact trans people's experiences uniquely and with particular violence. There are experiences that trans people share and others that we don't. Our rich community deserves a book for every story; this is only mine.

Introduction

It was a cold morning in November, and I was standing on the platform at Kilburn Tube station. I was in a rush. I was going somewhere. It was early and it was freezing. I hadn't worn a warm enough coat, and I was thinking about how I could barely feel my fingers and hoping that the Tube would come soon when my phone rang. It was an unknown number. I picked up because sometimes unknown numbers are important numbers. The person on the end of the line said, 'Hello, is this Tash?'

He introduced himself as someone living in the village I grew up in. I'd left many years ago, and I hadn't looked back. This man had heard I was trans and he'd heard I was happy now. He asked me if he could talk, and I said yes. He wanted to talk about his kid. His kid who was trans. He called me with a hope, a hope that I could tell him his kid would be okay.

So, I stood on that platform in the cold, I forgot about my Tube and where I was going, and I stopped to talk, because somebody needed to hear that trans people can have joy.

That dad's need to hear of trans joy, how hard I searched to find it and how easily it flourished when I did are the reasons I decided to write it all down.

Now this book is in your hands, I hope that it brings you joy too.

*

There wasn't a specific day when I woke up and realized that I was trans. Although I did know from a young age that being a girl was not something that came naturally to me – I wasn't good at it. I remember attending a Christmas party at a local zoo. The parents were asked to fill in a form with their children's names so that there would be a toy for each child. I saw a pink box for the girls and a blue box for the boys. When my name was called, I noticed my gift came from the blue box. My mum, knowing how deeply I would hate to receive a Barbie or a make-up set, had filled in the form to say I was a boy and that I would be picking a toy from the blue box of gifts. I remember this very clearly because it was one of the first times that I discovered that you could pick from a different box, and that you could act inside a box that wasn't necessarily the one you had been given. And later, that perhaps the boxes weren't really what I wanted at all. I've been exploring ever since.

The exploring has been excruciatingly painful at times. I spent years feeling alone and afraid, full of grief and shame. Then I grew up in the UK as a trans person. It feels like I have grown almost in tandem with the rise in transphobia. Every day that I embrace a little more of myself, of my transness, there is another law, another debate, another pushback against what it is to be trans.

Even as a trans person with enormous privilege, the violence of it is relentless. It is embedded. It is the death threats, the man who follows my partner home, the conversion therapy. It is a quarter of us experiencing homelessness,[1] it is when a friend is made to sign a 'morality clause' when renting a flat and it is how we take down our flags when the landlord comes to visit. It is the friend who steals cheese from the supermarket to get by, it is the almost stranger who sleeps on our sofa because there is nowhere else for him to go, it is the emergency care system we have in place because the health service lets us down. It is creating groups to safeguard our friends who are sex workers because labour laws and the state don't protect them.

It is half of us hiding who we are at work, one in eight of us being physically attacked by a colleague or customer in our jobs,[2] it is when a friend is fired for

---

1   Stonewall (2018) LGBT in Britain – Trans Report. www.stonewall.org.uk/lgbt-britain-trans-report
2   Stonewall (2018) LGBT in Britain – Trans Report. www.stonewall.org.uk/lgbt-britain-trans-report

being trans and the lady from Universal Credit tells them that other people have it worse. It is healthcare that requires years of unsupported waiting, creating a system where true access is only available with enormous costs. It is the way that I have learned to read and categorize the number plates, makes and colours of cars that pass me, in case their drivers shout abuse again.

It is all the things that made me delay coming out, the things that made me think that a trans life was inevitably a miserable, lonely and deeply undesirable one.

All of that was so overwhelming that I never knew there was anything else that being trans could be. But now I do.

I am a deep believer in joy. There are so many stories of transness that centre unhappiness. Transphobia holds so much power over our lives that it often becomes the main event. It can sometimes feel as if oppression and joy cannot coexist, that joy is a luxury, something we can't afford. While I was writing this, a wise friend reminded me why joy is so powerful. He said, 'Joy is different to happiness insofar as it is kinda non-dependent on circumstance.' That is something I learned in practice from him too. Even in the worst and bleakest material circumstances, there can be joy. Even under great threat, at the hands of systemic violence and harm, while suffering deep personal trauma and pain, joy manages to make space for itself.

When I sit down and remember all the ways that we have resisted, all of the ways we have lived and lost, I actually think joy is everything that keeps us here. It is the cracks that start to show in the structures that keep us out, it is the exhalation in a room of trans people when you let out a breath you didn't even know you had been holding, it is the sheer possibility contained within us and among us. It is growing and bringing others along with you, it is the collective. It is being always on the journey and never quite finished. Joy is integral to my trans experience; it is the part of me that believed my life could be different, the part of me that carries my body into the streets to protest injustice, the part of me that I am most proud of.

I do not think that joy is a luxury. In fact, I would go so far as to say that it is utterly essential. Trans joy is the part of the resistance that just keeps existing. It is what birthed Trans Pride and makes the numbers of trans people marching there swell every year. It is the thing that those who hate us most fear and are most powerless against. It is the transcendent part of us that cannot be taken, for nobody owns it.

It is our biggest power, in our lives and in this fight.

Transition isn't a before and after for me. I don't

think it is something that will ever be finished, partly because I don't think it is something that is happening just to me. The word 'trans' means across or beyond. I think transition happens across communities, across relationships, in solidarity. My becoming is interlinked with the becoming of those around me. I think trans people are beyond. Beyond most of the world's understanding. We go above and beyond for each other, with each other.

My aunt Kate once told me that we are pioneering. My first thought when she said that was that we are not new, we are not the first, we could not be pioneers. But perhaps it can all be true. We are history and the future, we are ahead of this time and yet we are returning to something ancient, something that generations of fearful people have tried to repress, something as inevitable as the turn of the season. We are that yellowed leaf that signals autumn's arrival, the first chill that climbs inside your bones and opens the door for winter, the very first peeping snowdrops of spring, the pulling of summer to the sky with the first day that the sun truly blazes. We are them all at once, always driving, always pushing things to grow and change, always gloriously, achingly beautiful. Always on our way, across and beyond.

You might expect most transition stories to be told in chronological order, from start to finish. But transition has not been something linear for me; my joy has come in seasons. Therefore, that is how I will tell my story here.

Autumn

Autumn is deep orange and ochre and brown. It is late September days with surprising sunshine and last warmth for shorts, morphing into October's big grandad jumpers and warm woollen socks. It is hot chocolate with marshmallows. It is breaking out the bobble hats and friends knitting you chaotic scarves. It is pumpkins and tea lights and movie evenings with popcorn. It is fireworks and sparklers in November. It is blankets and fleeces and layers. I love it.

Magic

I was born in the autumn, right after Bonfire Night. A firework baby. I used to love watching the colours and lights in the dark sky. My favourite was one that bloomed out from its top point like a mushroom, creating a dome of sparkling tails below. I've just looked it up; it's called a willow firework. We used to go watch them for my birthday. I loved the hushed excitement and the countdown before the explosions started. Shimmering booms of yellow and red and green. I remember my dad carefully explaining that fireworks were simple chemistry: sodium salts and burning metals. To me, though, they were pure magic.

I always loved magic. When I turned five, I had a magic party, and again when I was six, and seven, and eight. I fell in love with books about wizards and mystical creatures, benevolent trees, comrades met on the road, small moments of kindness that later turned out to create loyalties that saved the day. I imagined myself as one of those characters – I felt different to people around me. I wanted to have that moment where it would be revealed that actually I truly was different and now I was to be whisked off for an important adventure that would explain my destiny. It turned out that moment never came, but I did find my comrades on the road, and my own particular brand of magic.

In this country, there is a long history of queerness being seen as something to fear, to fight. A contagion of perversion and disgust. A history filled with people who have tried to control us, eradicate us, 'fix' us. We have been sinners, we have been criminals, we have been a sickness. This fear, and the laws and violence that accompany it, have been exported across the globe. This export has distorted cultures and communities where gender diversity has held a richness, a reverence, an honour, something beyond.

And yet still, this history of harm is one that shows we have always been here, always resisting.

I have found queerness to be a form of magic. It can be powerful, something to treasure, a gift. I was told that my queerness was wrong, sinful even. This book is full of evidence that this was never true. That thinking beyond, existing in the betwixt space, challenging the rigidity of the world, is magic in itself. We are not a mistake, we are not a defect or a biological hiccough. They call us a 'phase' because they think it makes us weak. But a phase isn't weak, it is change. A phase is a stage in a time of change, a moment of development.

We are evolution.

Coming Out

Transition is often portrayed in the singular, in the personal. An overcoming of our personal fears, a conquering and taming of our own bodies, a leashing and releasing of our own shames. It is the posting of progress photos, delicate writings that describe how a body is changing, voice recordings that document the individual ceremony of a transposing register over the days, the months, the years. These diaries of change, these sacred texts and artworks, these snippets of sound that capture the joy of finding your own voice are like a sacrament. These are the spaces where I first found words that spoke to my experience. It wasn't until later that I found that transition is also a collective, a library, a choir. My own personal shame, my own creating and overcoming, is a postage stamp in the collage of us. One that took me somewhere so that I could become something new.

When I came out as trans at 24, it was my second coming out. I'd come out as queer years earlier.

At 21, I buy my first binder. I tear open the parcel and try to pull the incredibly tight fabric over my head. I get stuck halfway and can't breathe for a minute, completely trapped. When I free myself and take the binder off again, I catch sight of my body in the mirror. The trapped feeling doesn't go away; in fact, it is often there alongside a constant acute awareness of the wrongness of my chest. I remember being a small kid on the beach and seeing men wandering about in their trunks, chests bare. I distinctly remember thinking, 'That's the sort of girl I will be when I grow up.' With some help from an online forum, I discover how to step into the binder and pull it up over my chest. I run my hands over the now reduced shape of my body and shut my eyes. Somehow, in a material that is compressing my entire top half, the tightness in my chest eases.

I know how my chest looks in my mind. It is flat and I can feel my sternum in the centre; my spine is straight without the shame weighing it down. I laugh with my chest wide open like my mouth. I hug tightly and properly, without fear. When I begin to dream it, it is like breaking the floodgates, and all I can do is think about it. It manifests itself as a constant occupation in my mind, taking up so much room that some things stop working in there. I can't swim any more, I can't look in mirrors or buy new clothes, I can't dance. At first, I run at night so that others can't see me, and then so that I can't even see myself. Later I stop running altogether. I start to shower in the dark then, unable to even touch parts of my body. My chest doesn't seem to belong to me, it sits upon me, making it hard to breathe. I find out that this is called dysphoria.

The binder gives me respite. It lets me wear that shirt that I love so much. It lets me smile and see my friends and get up every day. It is a snatch of quiet. It is a lifeline. It is also exhausting and painful and a burden. I keep it hidden, both my chest and who I am, and when I turn 24, I wear it for the last time.

Making that decision seemed to change everything. When I made the choice to listen to the heart of me, I went against so many voices that said I was making a mistake. Voices that said that I would be lonely, that I would regret it all, that I should wait that bit longer to be sure. Voices in every newspaper, in Parliament, built into our healthcare system.

I remember that moment reaching out like a fork in the road. It was bigger than whether I got the surgery or not, bigger than a yes or no answer. I knew that particular turn would affect every decision in my life, that denying myself the path I so desperately desired would mean turning my back on the courage to live my own life. It would mean shutting myself out, or in, or even off altogether. That decision was about letting go of pretending, choosing for myself, becoming.

I distinctly remember standing in the kitchen, slightly tipsy from a drink after work, and creating an alternative in my head. One where I was cis and I lived my life as a girl, a woman. It was all there, laid out.

But it was all make-believe.

And even with the haziness of alcohol at the edges, I couldn't make myself believe.

I Dance for the First Time

A few years ago, my gorgeous friend Pod made a New Year's resolution to 'embrace the cringe'. I spent a lot of time thinking about the idea of 'the cringe'. It is that burning hot feeling that creeps over your scalp; it makes your skin tight and you want to run. We are taught to feel it when people are expressing themselves in a way that feels too big for us – spoken word, dancing, karaoke, wrong notes. The cringe comes when we see that very particular brand of self-expression that is exposing, vulnerable-making, too much. Kids don't have the cringe; they learn it, we all do. It steals our childlike courage and limits us. As far back as I can remember, I have felt an intense level of self-consciousness around myself, my actions, my existence. I would feel this to such a level that it leaked into other things. When Pod started to embrace the cringe, I realized that the cringe is essential. It is how we get vulnerable with people; it is part of loving and being true to ourselves. The cringe, that was once something I could not stand, has now become something I embrace. I love people who dance with complete abandon, who sing at the top of their voice, who try new things. Before I came out, the cringe was so deep in every part of me that I couldn't really live how I wanted. Every day now I let the cringe in, and my life is so much sillier, so full of joy, so much bigger than before.

That golden sun of autumn's first days is there when I dance for the first time. I am 26 years old, and I have never before danced like I do that day. Every year I watch my siblings dance, heads tipped back, completely absorbed, happy. Every year I watch and wish that I could dance as I shuffle my feet and watch our coats and bags. Finally, this day, I move with them. In a field. Under a canopy of canvas, the music blares. My siblings stand up, and this time I let go of carrying shame and the self-consciousness I have worn since I can remember, and I abandon our belongings in the grass. My chest open, eyes bright, I turn and jump and let the music in. It is a power like being on fire, and I can't stop moving. My body aches like it has waited a lifetime for this moment, and it has. Our bodies are a blur, but I can still see the pride radiating from my siblings' faces. I am laughing and then I might be crying, because I am dancing and in all those years of watching and yearning, I never knew it felt like this.

It's not just dancing that I discover; lots of things are cringe. Love is cringe! (Exclamation marks are really cringe!) Letting your guard down, telling someone your feelings, being your truest self. It is all cringe, excruciatingly so at times. But embracing it meant that when I met Seren, I didn't close up, I didn't play it safe. At the end of our first date, I asked them if I could kiss them. (One hundred per cent cringe, one hundred per cent an excellent kiss.) We talked for hours about names and our lives and gender and penguins. They played me a song on their guitar; I fell in love.

Before Seren, I felt like I had to make up for my transness by being the best partner I could be, as if my transness was something to be mitigated. I was so wrong. Being trans is not something I need to diminish; it is what pushes me to imagine, to create, to build. We are dreamers and makers because that is how we forged ourselves. Coming out, embracing the cringe, nurturing joy, have all made being in a relationship so vibrant, so full of goodness.

Today, when Seren reads this, they begin to cry and say, 'I never knew you didn't dance. Our third date you danced so beautifully with me. You made me feel safe.' And then I am crying too, because of dancing and third dates and making each other feel safe.

Max and Lynne

We often speak of the 'trans community' as if it is a locatable, definable group. Some even see it as an organized activist movement with leaders and actions and an agenda. Our will to exist is seen as activism, and it is, but not in the way that they think it is. I have read comments from anti-trans commentators where they express their confusion that our 'meetings' take place in small, scattered groups, that we have no obvious leaders, but that despite this, somehow unity is still achieved.

Earlier I described transition as a library. I learn from so many different parts of the library. My story could fit in multiple sections. There are books with the same title and yet wildly different narratives. We find shared experience in a line from one, and disagree over a line from another. I will never read every book here, but they are all here nonetheless, full of possibility. We are not a monolith. This community is fluid, breathing, ever creating and re-creating. We form pockets of together-ness in a thousand ways: through a nod in the street with a stranger, the GoFundMe donation to a friend of a friend, in the comments section on a coming-out post, a charged moment on the dancefloor, a glance across a clinic waiting room. There is a transience to the building of these moments, a temporary nature that creates and then gently dismantles community in the time it takes to dip one's chin. And then there are the moments we build with those who we bring close: the sacredness of a goodnight forehead kiss, the sharing of childhood stories, the vulnerability of 3 a.m. truths. We carry them with us, a community that cannot be contained.

In September we go to visit Max and Lynne by the coast. We can't touch because of the virus. I want to hug Lynne, the sort of hug that says, 'Hello. Welcome to the family, I can't wait to know you.' I want to hug Max, the sort of hug that says, 'Hello. I've missed you, dear one. Let's hold on a little longer.' Instead, we stand awkwardly outside at the back of their house and talk from at least two metres apart about how fun it is to squirt dog shit off the patio tiles with a pressure hose.

We drive to get Subways, and when we get out in the car park Seren gently bumps the next car with their door. A man gets out to shout. Later Max tells us that while we were queuing, Lynne gave that man hell for yelling at us. Something hot and strong burns in my chest at that. At the speed with which we trust, at the strength with which we lean in to love, at the fierceness of us to protect one another.

We walk some empty streets. A friend joins with her pony and we lead it down a track where we stumble upon a field of sunflowers. It is so strangely wonderful it might be a scene from a movie. Sun blazing down on us, casting the shadows of five trans people and a pony.

Later, tents up and beers in hand, we talk. About horses, about acrylic nails, about a friend who was arrested in Dubai for their passport, for being trans. We talk about being one of us in a seaside town. We talk about relationships, and I think about what has brought the two of them together, and now all of us.

We sit around the campfire and the wood is spitting out sparks that dance in front of my eyes. Fire has always been captivating to me, and the cold of the night draws us all in close. We seem to breathe with the flames, laughing and joking loudly, and then there are moments of quiet when the logs smoulder. It feels magical, the dark and the light and my friends. Max and Lynne are sitting in camping chairs. They are both wrapped up warm in blanket hoodies, their knees just touching. I am looking at them across the red heat of the blaze, and something about the gentleness of the point where their knees touch, the softness of the chairs, the casualness of it all, makes me think of my grandparents.

I wake early in the morning and turn to Seren, my bones aching from a night on hard ground. Their cheeks are so rosy they glow and for a while I just marvel. We get up and have a cup of tea and a Pot Noodle for breakfast. Last night's magic has faded into something more solid, a community of sorts. We pack up as a unit, cleaning our teeth over the grass and unpegging tents. We drive to the sea. It is the same sea where I swam with Max before. Two Novembers back, shirt stripped off, I ran into the ocean flat-chested for the first time. It is like the water remembers me, the cold bite and rush of life in my bones. Afterwards, just like the first time, my scars turn pink and we drink hot chocolate with marshmallows, our wet hair sticking up. This time Seren is there too, eating a chocolate ice cream as big as their head. Both times we are the only ones swimming. In November, people dressed in scarves and gloves looked at us like we were crazy. This time it is September, but they still look at us.

We just tip our heads back like gulls and grin.

Swimming Again

When our bodies are policed, it hurts. It excludes us and keeps us from our joy. I have always been uncomfortable in a changing room, but now it is near impossible. First, I have to choose which violence to face: I am more likely to get thrown out if I use the women's, but using the men's is a threat I have lived with my whole life. Sometimes I chance going in. I start with the women's, head down, movements quick, avoiding others. One time I stand in the shower for an extra 20 minutes until my fingertips wrinkle up, waiting for the voices to quiet so I know the coast is clear. After a while I am being asked to leave on almost every occasion, so I switch to the men's. Mostly though, I avoid these spaces entirely. I turn down invitations, I change at home, I hold it rather than pick a toilet to use. I have friends who have experienced chronic UTIs as a result of this. I know people who have been threatened.

Years ago, I remember reading a long thread on Twitter that asked the following question: What would you do as a trans person if there was no transphobia for one day? It produced a heartbreaking and joyous mix of responses, from wearing a favourite pink dress, to coming out, to trying a new lipstick, to playing sport. But the thing that kept coming up again and again was to swim. To swim in a pool with friends, to swim on holiday and soak up the sun, to jump into the ocean and gasp with the cold of it. So many voices that said if they had that day, they should just like to swim.

One Friday night we gather in a swimming pool in Lewisham. It is a special night where they close the pool so that only trans people can use the session and we can swim in peace. In the changing rooms we take off our day wear. Something stiff and old in me wants to be self-conscious, of my body and this small space and all the unspoken shame that lives in my shoulder blades. But then someone catches my eye. They are wearing a business suit and smart black shoes. We link eyes just as they pull down the drab grey, revealing the most magnificent pink dress beneath. The edges of pink tulle skirts burst free of the belt strap and my eyes light in surprise. I smile, they smile back. There is power in the grey suit and smart shoes, a power that keeps us ambiguous, acceptable, perhaps sometimes safe. But there is also the power of a hidden pink dress, a delicious knowing of who you are. And then, finally, there is the reveal: a metamorphosis that only some are lucky enough to witness. Today I am gifted that, and the courage of that moment spills into the space in a way that feels contagious. The air is charged with it, like a husk of discomfort has been shelled off with our clothes. Our bodies are all different, and yet, for one of the first times in my life, I don't feel ashamed to undress.

In the water, we can be just us. Our bodies and our swimming wear accepted. I don't hunch or drag my shoulders inwards; I float. It strikes me how infrequently I get to do this, to open my chest and let my shoulder blades rest weightlessly on the water. The pool becomes a sanctuary of sorts. There is some talk of transness; recommendations for surgeons and advice about various medical issues are exchanged. As we tread water and talk, strangers become temporary friends.

Then, as if the water has made us all lighter, we seem to collectively let go. A friend carries Freddy like a baby in their arms. They sing a song together as they walk through the water, caught in their own moment. River gives me a piggyback and we fall into the water laughing. Our bodies are not out of place or observed, just living and breathing and laughing – joyful in fact. My chest swells with the ease of it. I don't know if the lifeguard recognizes a need in us, or if they have been told to do what happens next, but it is exactly the right thing when they pull out the floats. There are those pool noodles that you can balance on, and blow-up balls, and big square platform floats. It is a moment when I feel the air change, the excitement to play. Because so much of being trans is made to be so serious, a struggle, a need to explain and to stand your ground again and again. That evening we don't have to do any of that. People clamber on the floats and wobble on the noodles and throw the balls at one another, squealing with laughter like little kids when someone is capsized. It is the sort of playing that heals something inside you without you even knowing. I climb out of the water a little taller.

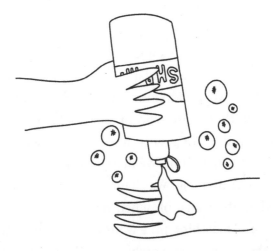

We share out shampoo when we go to shower, tiny moments of care offered into open palms. Later, hair still wet, we part ways into the night, but the bubble of joy and the floats and the secret pink dress stay with me long after.

Trans Pride

Coming out didn't stop after the first, or the second time. I still have to come out now, sometimes multiple times a day. Sometimes people don't understand or they ask entirely inappropriate questions and say all the wrong things. But sometimes they surprise you.

The sun is blazing and it is the first ever Trans Pride in London. We are anxious on the Tube, afraid of the disruption that those who oppose us have promised. We keep quiet, biting nails, heads down. But when we reach the start, it is full. We march through London and people cheer us along. We chant at the top of our voices, 'Oh when the trans, oh when the trans, oh when the trans come marching in, I want to be in that number, when the trans come marching in.' And I realize quite suddenly that it is true, I finally want to be in that number, I am in that number and I'm surrounded by people I love.

Freddy is wearing a dress and we wave flags over our heads, me and Max wearing ours as capes. Somebody sets up a speaker in Soho Square and blasts out 'What's Up' by 4 Non Blondes. We sing along, eyes bright with it. There are people with artworks painted on their faces, there are joyous bodies dancing furiously, dressed as if they have just walked out of New York Fashion Week. We stare at each other, taking in the colour and swirl of vibrant fabrics, the audacity of the outfits. The stares are holy, reverent even.

My best friend, Adam, has come along to support. I feel a deep swell of pride sharing this community with him. He squeezes my hand as if to tell me he sees it all too – the magic of us. Sometimes you have to explain to people how to be in your space. Sometimes you have to explain to people who aren't trans how to speak and move and take up space with trans people. But not this day with Adam. He moves with us, without taking up space. And when we become a group of six as the last dancers faded into the day, when our bellies groan, he stays. We walk to get noodles. Some strangers, some friends, some brand-new connections. Sitting at the table, we talk and laugh and eat ramen until refuelled. And then quietly, Adam excuses himself for the toilet. When he returns the whole bill is paid.

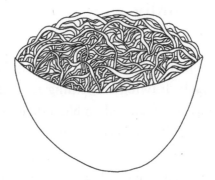

I don't think he knew the impact or the importance of that moment, didn't know that for some of us that was one hot and happy meal in a week of hunger. But he understood something vital that day about how to care for a community, about how to say thank you, about the gift of sharing a meal and a march and a day. When we said thank you, he said it was his honour to have shared with us, to have been allowed into a piece of our magic.

As I fall asleep, there is a glow in my chest that has become as familiar as the tightness used to be, a feeling I didn't know before and one that I now treasure: to be seen.

Chosen Family

Recently someone asked me to draw my family tree. I found myself drawing something new. It wasn't a lineage family tree focussed on blood lines, but instead it looked more like the cross-section of a tree trunk where you can see all the rings. I recall being taught that the rings in a tree trunk each symbolize a year of growth. This is how I reimagine my family tree today: a series of concentric circles with names squeezed between the lines, crossing multiple rings, some pushing out to the edges.

You can tell so many things by looking at those rings in a tree. You can tell when they began to grow, and when they were leaned on by other trees and had to grow in a new direction. You can tell when they struggled to compete with their neighbours for sunshine and water, and when they had the space to breathe again. You can tell when the environment was too dry, or when insects invaded and slowed their growth. You can even see the tree's scars, perhaps from forest fire, and where the new layers of wood covered them up. I like to think that you can see all that in my family tree. All the times I was leaned upon, and all the times my environment stopped me thriving. I especially like to think about all of those people who were essential in the growing of me across all my years and how those rings would never have formed in the same way without them. Those people, those names that I write into my rings, are not about lineage and shared blood, but something more. They are my chosen family.

Like the strong and ancient growth of a tree, I have acquired the most wonderful trans family. Formed from chance meetings, message boards, snail mail and vulnerability, my rings have filled with names.

Some I know for years before they come out, some I meet as they are exploring who they are, some I seek out on my own journey. I meet Xan at med school and they are assigned to be my mentor, then years later I drop out and we both come out. They are there to drive me to the airport for surgery, to my first time back in a swimming pool, to my new home with all my belongings. Freddy and Max are old friends turned best friends. Freddy's paintings adorn the walls of all the places I live, their vibrancy inspires my courage to exist in my body, to create, to dance. Max's embroideries hang by my mirror, reminding me of the goodness in me and why we keep fighting, fists in the air. River and I can never quite decide where we first met but have shared a uni and a home. We also share dreams, and they teach me about relationships and courage and resilience. I make some friends online and we share our hopes and fears via text. P helps me with translations when I start to learn Welsh. We haven't met in person yet but they send a parcel of art and chocolate and zines in the post to make me happy. We send snippets of our days to each other for years. When their cat passes away, I light a candle and grieve a little too. Otto is the one who guides me through surgery, takes me to football games, sends me plants to fill my home. I meet Eddy at work and they become my rock, filling my days with understanding and compassion.

These friends expand my circles, they bring new people, too many to list though all essential to my growing, like a forest of interconnected roots and stretching branches: across and beyond.

One day we talk about it; Seren asks me why chosen family is so different, so unique. I tell them that I think it is because queer and trans people often have a hard time growing up and relationships feel fragile. When we find people who love us and accept all of us, we hold on tighter. We have so much love to give. I never thought I would have chosen family like this. I hope that if you are reading this waiting for your people, you feel a part of this chosen family, this book, this joy.

Samhain

I don't even know what Samhain is until we are arranging to meet for it. It looks like it may rain so we club together and buy a gazebo. We arrive from all our different places, and we put it up in Flori's garden and string coloured fairy lights around all the poles. Everyone's faces glow with green and pink and blue. Freddy makes a vat of Samhain stew and it is the best thing I've tasted. We wolf it down with bread and follow up with sweet things and endless cups of tea. The air is frosty and we are wrapped in scarves and woolly jumpers. Me and Seren present everyone with tiny envelopes. Each contains a foraged leaf in autumn colours, two scraps of paper and a penny dated with their birth year. It's a ritual we have entirely made up, but everyone loves it. We write things we want to let go of on one scrap, and things we are grateful for on another. A quietness falls around us, the coloured glow on the tent walls and the shared space within feels safe and warm despite the chill. Some people share their words in the circle, words of community, of togetherness, of struggle and solidarity. Big, rich words like joy, transformation, forgiveness, family. Words I didn't know were allowed to be mine but that taste so right in my mouth. And then we burn the papers with a lighter in our hands, dropping them into a bowl of water for the ash to cool. The calm is broken by laughter when some barely light, floating in the water instead. As night draws in, we part ways and the gazebo is put away for another day. On the way home we spot a building with its name 'CIS Security' glowing in bright blue luminescence. We take a photo and laugh from our bellies.

SAMHAIN STEW IN 3 STEPS

INGREDIENTS:

2 x TINS OF TOMATOES
1 x ONION
3 x GARLIC CLOVES
VEGGIE STOCK
TEASPOON OF PAPRIKA
PINCH OF CHILLI FLAKES
SOME SPRIGS OF FRESH HERBS:
THYME + ROSEMARY
2 x BAY LEAVES
A GLUG OF APPLE CIDER VINEGAR
KALE
SWEET POTATO
SQUASH
SAUSAGES OF YOUR CHOICE

STEP 1:

CHOP ALL VEG, GARLIC + ONION + ADD TO BIG CAULDRON WITH OIL. STIR FOR 5 MINS ON MEDIUM HEAT.

STEP 2:

ADD TINNED TOMATOES, VEGGIE STOCK, HERBS, SPICES + APPLE CIDER VINEGAR.
STIR + LEAVE TO SIMMER FOR A COUPLE OF HOURS.

STEP 3:

COOK SAUSAGES, CHOP INTO CHUNKS + ADD TO CAULDRON.
SERVE HOT WITH CRUSTY BREAD.

Winter

Winter is icy blue and white and grey. It is December frost and fairy lights. It is the smell of pine and cinnamon. It is fresh clementines and thick winter coats with deep pockets. It is board games and the same red childhood stocking hung on the fireplace. It is fingerless gloves from my aunt every year at Christmas. It is January blues and big boots for walking. It is February and new, stiff jeans. It is cold and crisp and chunky. I love it.

Insurance Systems

The winter months are long and cold, and often sparse. We become each other's insurance systems by some sort of tacit agreement. I take some extra-long shifts at the hospital and cover River's rent for a bit. I come home exhausted and we huddle on the sofa eating Mexican food and watching TV. On the days I am weary, Freddy sends poems and photos of frost on the trees. He gets himself in debt trying to keep alive and creative, and I meet him after some months apart at a corner curry café in New Cross. We eat vegetable curry and dhal and work out a plan.

On a back table of a central London Pret, we start budgeting on scraps of paper. Over filter coffee we call his phone company and negotiate a better deal. Weeks later we make a call in Wetherspoons to sort out his council tax. We share chips and we cheer when they agree to waive the fines. Slowly we pay off the debts and it doesn't feel like a chore, it feels like winning.

We go for pancakes, thick and loaded with toppings. River joins us and we talk about dysphoria and chin hairs and utopia. Then we walk around in the rain and buy some minoxidil; we share the bottles out in the street and promise to send photos of any facial hair growth. Me and Freddy head to the National Portrait Gallery and we walk around pointing out the paintings of ancient royalty that we pretend are queer, capes and ruffs and full drag glory. When we leave we walk past some street graffiti; it is a white Sharpie scribble that says 'end violence against trans people'. We stop in the drizzle and take photos with it.

Because ending violence against trans people is bigger than the threats and the headlines and the being spat at in the street. The violence is not being able to access healthcare, not being able to afford our rent, being forced out of our homes, jobs, places of worship. The way we care for each other feels like some sort of yearning to stop the violence. As if being as gentle as we can will stop some of the pain, as if the solidarity of softness can be a shield against the violence.

The three of us spend more time together after that. Meeting at Maggie's Café in Lewisham where she makes us the biggest plates of hearty food. We marvel at the portions. Six pounds ninety-five for a king-sized veggie curry, the sort that comes with a gravy boat of extra sauce. She brings over a pot of mango chutney with a spoon and wanders round the warm space with her arms full of an enormous teapot. Maggie won't let your cup go empty and she'll never charge you extra for it either; she knows how to feed you up for the fight.

The night of the general election, when I arrive home after a day of knocking doors and talking to voters, when my feet are aching and face chapped with wind, when the exit poll comes out and my heart breaks clean in two, they both arrive. I don't even ask, they just turn up, knock on the door and take me to my room. We take it in turns to cry into each other with the fear and devastation and rage of such an important loss. The three of us eat oven chips out of a Pyrex dish and the saltiness is a balm to our tears. We squeeze into the tiniest single bed and hold each other. When the morning comes, we sing Billy Bragg songs at the top of our voices and cook up a breakfast of kings. The sun is shining and something in the togetherness sticks a splinter of hope into the day.

Hope: Trying Is Good

I have spent long periods of my life feeling hopeless, like nothing could change. When I look back now, I can see that I survived all of these times by trying anyway. I didn't always believe that I could change things, but I kept trying. I never thought I could be happy, but I kept moving as if one day it might happen.

Trying helped me come out of the closet, trying helped me have courage to curate my body, trying brought me friends, family, a future. And finally, many years later, trying led to hope.

It is a freezing cold Friday night and we are walking the streets in protest. It is something we have done a hundred times before, for the planet, against wars, for queer rights, against welfare cuts, for trans rights, against racism and police brutality. Today there are more police than I can count. We raise our voices and take it in turn to lead chants. When one voice starts to shake, another rises up to take the call. When we make our way into the centre of the city, they kettle us. They accidentally trap a London bus full of commuters in the process. Shouts of 'Free the bus' lift over the crowd. We sit on the concrete, huddling together for warmth. A pal comes over and teaches us protest law on the floor. There is a young boy near us who is scared. We invite him over with a space to sit. A bag of tiny clementines is passed around. There is something so intimate about sharing

out the segments of orange, a snack so small yet still divided. It tastes all the sweeter for it.

Transgiving

December is dark, and it is hard to get out of bed some mornings. One day I am talking with Seren about the worst days, when I sat with my coat and gloves on in my bedroom, unhappy and eating peanut butter straight from the jar with a spoon. We share the stories of the bleakness of winters gone, and how grateful we are for our community and how they got us through those times. We want to give something back now. Transgiving is born.

One hundred and fifteen people sign up for a winter care package from us. Trans people from all over send us artwork; glorious stacks of prints pile up in our flat. There are keyrings and stickers and postcards and exquisite ceramic bowls. There are socks and scented candles and badges and enamel pins. We potato print brown paper to wrap the gifts in and package them up with hot chocolate sachets and winter teas, sweets and chocolate coins, soaps and coasters and seeds to grow sunflowers. We go over to Lizzie's house and spend a whole evening making bracelets with each person's name on them. The floor of our flat becomes a production line and scraps of paper with the names of this new trans family are placed all across the floor as we create each gift. We tiptoe between the rows and add new goodies to each pile. It takes three days to wrap them all. Each night after work we pick up the ribbon and tape and begin again.

When they are all labelled, we slip the presents into discreet black mail bags. Many of these gifts are going to people who are not safe to be out, people who need a different name on the outside to the one that is truly theirs. Our friends Tilly and Flora help us send the international parcels out to France and South Dakota and California and Thailand and Canada and all across the world. We divide the last packages and hit every post office in town. It takes four hours to get the whole lot sent. When people receive them, we get the most wonderful messages back. For many people it is the only gift, or the only affirming gift, that they receive. The creativity of our community opened in homes all over the world. Someone in the USA reads about the project and asks to set up their own version in the States. The joy spreads.

It feels like our family stretches wider now. Creating these bundles of love and joy for strangers somehow makes them feel like friends.

And then there is a message that comes after all the others, a message that makes us cry, a message that says, 'Thank you for making me feel trans enough.'

Isaac

I used to think nothing good could come from January. I hated New Year; it felt like a day just to remind me that another year had passed where I was unhappy. Things started to change over the years. We started a tradition of games night and copious amounts of food. My sister's friend Isaac would come over and we would play board games until we couldn't keep our eyes open. Soon he was my friend too. Often, we would run into the street in the dark and walk, just because we could. Isaac would stay over and snore so loudly that we would all giggle silently. He was the first person I watched come out as trans and thrive, the first glimpse of trans joy.

Years of games later and the messages between Isaac and me have become an alternation between discussion of TV shows we both love and top surgeon choices. I talk with him about transness many times; he helps me buy my first binder, get my first referral to a gender clinic. When dysphoria becomes unbearable, it is Isaac I message first, and again when my referral is accepted. He always tells me to go for what I want, so I do.

Sureness Is a Trap

The medical system in the UK demands many things of trans people. I personally spent years considering my gender quietly. I didn't speak about it aloud much because I knew that to be trans was to be unhappy; that is what I had been told. I confessed it occasionally, to a changing room curtain, to my bedroom mirror, to myself. But I never let it become real. I held it off, like a coat I really wanted to try on but knew I would have to buy if I let myself see how good it looked on me. Over time it seemed to seep out of me, small slivers that friends noticed, less like a coming out, more of a spilling out. When I booked that first appointment at the GP I realized it had never been a coat that I had been wanting to try on, it was more like there was something that I needed to take off. When I took that thing off, when I saw what was underneath, putting it back on felt like deceit.

The doctor thought I might need to see a psychiatrist, but I knew that a referral to a gender clinic did not require such a thing. In fact, the community had prepared me for this moment. As I sat down in that clinic room, the voices and advice of a hundred trans siblings backed me up. They had sent me prepared with printouts of healthcare guidance and information. I knew the referral process better than the doctor himself. I'm not exaggerating – he told me I did. I spent years putting off the moment of referral because I wanted to be sure before I did it. Then, when I finally found the courage, I was not just ready, I was desperate. The NHS gender specifications use the word 'timely' 14 times, yet when I finally received my letter they told me that the wait would be 12–18 months. I managed three before I looked for care elsewhere.

R wants to go on testosterone; they've wanted it for a while. So we talk about it, we all do. They come over and we all sit in our tiny kitchen, on stools and on the counters. We talk about what it would mean, about emotions and fears and partners. We talk about dysphoria and how their body will change, we look at pictures of how hormones will affect their genitalia – pictures that are hard to come by. R listens to several first-hand accounts of how T has affected people; we talk about it all. There is transparency and honesty and they think about it all, hard. It is a conversation we keep having, a community processing and learning and wondering together.

One afternoon we all congregate at the Kilburn flat. We make mugs of tea and sit around chatting. R has their post delivered here because theirs keeps being stolen, and a parcel has arrived for them in the mail. In it are vials and needles. Someone has provided advice about the safest place to buy hormones, another friend has bought a needle bucket and supplies and teaches R how to inject themself. We help them find the right spot and then watch as they take testosterone for the first time. The moment is a precious one, later dubbed the 'T party'. We point out the places where R can get their bloods checked and we keep them with us after, eating biscuits and checking they are okay. It all took a community to pull it off and the care provided is better than I have seen from most gender clinicians.

The gender clinics have abandoned us. We make our own way rather than let the death toll rise. We fund each other's healthcare, paying for private appointments, helping people access care abroad. We share and contribute to GoFundMe pages, the comments sections showing international support for our communities, from friends and from strangers. We attend each other's surgery consults, help each other arrange appointments and fill in forms. We message across our networks to self-source oestrogen. We have video calls with people who have just come out, meet their families and answer their questions. I lift my shirt countless times, let people touch my scars, let them ask about how it feels. Through the years we sit on never-ending waiting lists and in appointments where cis people decide whether we know ourselves. In a system that doesn't function, our community is our healthcare.

It is early January and I am sending photos of myself naked from the waist up to a man across the ocean. My desired surgeon wants to see what he is working with. I'm quite shocked when I see the pictures myself. I have managed to avoid seeing the reality of my body for many months and what I see is unexpected. Binding has pulled my shoulders in towards my chest, and my back hunches inwards, shrinking as much of me as is possible. The look on my face is so uncomfortable that I delete the photos and emails afterwards.

I put down a deposit that wipes clean my bank account. My sister Anna texts me: 'I have been thinking about how the op date is on the summer solstice, and how that feels like the rightest thing, and all the conversations we've had over all these years. Everything brave is the hardest thing you will ever do, and you have to see the part of yourself that desperately wants to be brave and just run in that direction as hard as you can. We are all here for you. If you're anxious for five months, fine. It's just anxiety. It's just courage. I trust you and I trust what you've always known.'

I save that message and read it whenever I feel bad, which is a lot. Because actually, anything brave in life is scary. Exploring gender is scary, surgery is scary, decisions are scary. I remember when I start to tell people about the fact that I will be flying across the ocean to have my chest cut up. Lots of them are afraid too. Lots of them want to know if I am sure, if I am certain that this will make me happy. That's where I start to become unstuck. Because transness to me is about exploring and fluidity and escape from all the structures of sureness. I do not know what it will feel like to be me after the operation, I cannot know, so of course I cannot be sure.

It seems that sureness is what the people want, it is the pass required to access transness. Doctors, family, strangers, they all want it. I must not express doubt, or nuance. I must be psychologist-certified sure. The sureness is essential actually, in a way that terrifies me. I become paralysed with the worry that I am not sure enough. I can't sleep or eat or work. The anxiety engulfs me entirely; I don't leave my bedroom for weeks. In the lulls I force myself to eat tiny pots of chocolate yoghurt, which is all I can stomach. I spend hours on the phone to Anna, often just repeating 'I can't do this' over and over like a prayer. She just sits and listens, often until I fall asleep. I so desperately want to be sure, to say I have one hundred per cent certainty forever until I die, but how can anybody be that sure of anything? I try to convince myself that actually I don't need surgery, I can pretend to be a girl for the rest of my life. It doesn't work.

The need to be sure makes me sick. My head spends every waking minute trying to find a sureness that feels airtight. I remind myself that on 99 days out of the last 100 my chest made me want to die, but that one day when I felt indifferent makes me not quite sure enough.

It is two weeks since I last left the house when I finally leave for a party. We get off the Tube and I run to the gutter where I retch; the sickness is in all of my body now. 'I can't do this,' I say, and at the time I think I am talking about going to the party, or getting the surgery, but now I know I am talking about finding that certainty everyone has been demanding of me. As I curve bent double in an alley off Cally Road, my phone rings. I pick up and my mum says to me, 'I've been trying to call you all day. I just had this feeling I needed to ring you, to tell you that it is all going to be okay.'

I don't know what it is about that phone call, why it seems to make all the difference, but it does. Because the thing is, sureness is a trap. Nobody can achieve the level of certainty that is demanded of us, not really, but any admission of this may be used in evidence against you. The sureness is a deterrent, it makes you too afraid to take action. It makes people too afraid to wonder, to explore, to try things out. It creates a world in which you can't trust your own body, your own thoughts, your own pain. It creates fear that stops you from finding you.

That fear stopped me from exploring. That fear meant I waited and waited and waited, searching for a sureness I would never find. I waited to admit the agony of my body, I waited to bind, I waited to use the term 'non-binary', I waited to use the pronouns I wanted, I waited to use the word 'trans'. I waited years to start living, and for many that wait is too long to hold out for.

In the end I never was one hundred per cent sure, but of course that was never going to be possible. For them sureness was safety, but for me sureness was another structure holding me back from what I could be. And the thing is, I wanted freedom. I wish I could say that I eventually trusted myself, that I stopped searching and walked into my decision fully ready. But the reality is that it wasn't until I sat in that hospital bay in Florida, and the surgeon drew his guidelines on my chest in felt tip, that my heart finally stilled. It wasn't until the moment, when I knew that the surgery was going to happen unless I stopped it, that I felt calm and the frenzy in my head ceased. It wasn't until I stopped fighting for what I wanted that I could truly feel ready for it to happen. And then...well, then I didn't care about what *they* wanted any more.

Today, I am happy. Not one hundred per cent of days of course. But I am truly, deeply happy, in a way I couldn't be before, in a way that still takes me by surprise. I am happy that I had courage, that I explored and continue to explore, that I dared to be me, truly and fully. I love my chest, I love my life, I love being trans. And of all these things, I am sure.

Seren

The first date I ever go on with Seren is in January. We meet in a pub in Islington and order vodka. They're quiet and I can't stop talking. They still let me have a second date. We walk through Hackney talking about everything. It is the sort of date you never want to end. Eventually we run out of road so we sit on a bench and edge closer and closer under the guise of the freezing night air. I have to go to babysit but we agree to meet the very next morning for coffee in the park. As we part I look back, my face split with a grin, my fingers numb with cold. That bench becomes the moment, the changing point. Days later I buy them a small soft penguin in a bookshop and surprise them with it. We kiss shyly, like we are still afraid of someone seeing what this might be. Afterwards I go home to look after my little cousin and we sit in bed chatting. She asks me about what transphobia is, and I explain to her. She nods her head quietly and takes it in solemnly in a way she has always done since she was so tiny. Then she climbs in next to me and hugs me tight.

Seren has a thing for greasy spoons and mapping out the best ones in London, so I take them to my favourite. I tell them about how this is where I sat after coming out to my GP, after break ups, after dropping out of uni. This is where I have come so many times for good eggs and solace. They seem to take on the importance of the New River Café because soon we are writing pro and con lists about life over cups of tea. We have been speaking for one month and yet when the list turns to leaving the city, moving miles away, I want to write my name down in the con list so badly. It's been a month, and yet, sitting with a mug of tea in my hands watching the morning pass by, I think I might follow them anywhere.

Freddy

February hits and the cold is in my bones. We are going to a poetry night and are meeting for food before. Freddy messages me at work: 'What time will you get to mine? Will we have time to cuddle before we go out? I'm tired and sad today.'

The sky is painted like the trans flag, pink, fluffy clouds on a blue backdrop as I trek over to South London. Inside we warm up from the heat of the stove as we cook pasta and meatballs in a big pan. The weight of the day falls off me as we dance; Freddy stands on my feet as I walk him around the kitchen. I watch him carefully as he adds the herbs and spices – paprika, basil, thyme. He throws them in in fistfuls, like a potion or a spell. It seems erratic but it smells perfect. He probably doesn't know it but it was him that taught me about spices and herbs. It was Freddy who taught me to add them confidently, to flavour well.

We keep coming back to each other as we stir the sauce. Backwards hugs and arm squeezes, deep inhales of tomatoey goodness. When we place the pan on the table, my heart has lightened and filled with warmth. The pan has the spaghetti and the meatballs in and Freddy has sprinkled twists of basil on the top.

It is colourful and beautiful and I love how it is all in the one pan.

Bellies full, we rush out of the door. We always seem to be running a little late, always too full of the previous activity to let go in time. We make it to a small room upstairs in a gloomy building. We creep in at the back and listen to a night of beautiful words. At the end we are standing and hugging close and a priest wanders over and leans in to us. 'God fucking loves you,' she says.

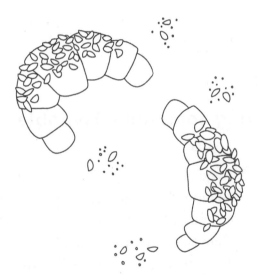

Afterwards we are brimming with a need to write, so we scramble to a coffee shop and order hot chocolate. It isn't quite hot enough to burn our mouths even as we gulp it down too fast. We scribble ideas in silence, and just before our pens begin to slow the server tells us they are closing soon. As we turn to leave, Freddy approaches the counter and asks about the pastries going to waste. I swallow the surprise in my mouth as they hand them over for free. We walk out with one each and I brush almond crumbs from my mouth as we walk back to the station, grinning with the delight of a surprise gift. I think it is pure magic, but Freddy just grins, mouth full of croissant, and says, 'Shy bairns get nowt.'

Curating Something Liveable

Xan, Freddy and I make a trip to the Serpentine Gallery to see an exhibition about gender. There are dripping pipes and acid rain falls onto a single gargoyle. There is a video of animals in a slaughterhouse. The art asks about the things that make some bodies liveable and others unliveable. When we leave the space we walk down to the river and get hot chocolate from a small kiosk. We sit on a bench and drink it while watching a pair of bright green parakeets fight over a branch. My body has felt unliveable: for years it was so full of sad that I wanted to tear it open to create space. Then it was so misaligned, so malfitting, I couldn't even feel the acid rain. Now though. Now there is the art inked on my skin, the scars that cross my chest like a smile, the places I have allowed hair to grow and the places I have cut it short. I have curated my body, and in doing so I have come to live in it again. And liveable still sometimes means pain and ache and heaviness, but it also means that sometimes I am so full of joy I think I might fly or my skin might spontaneously begin to glow. Liveable means that sometimes I might sit on a bench and drink a hot chocolate while laughing with my whole chest at two green parakeets.

The curation of a trans body is a community effort. We are a family, an ancestry of sorts. At the beginning I found Otto. We met online when I was scrolling through a trans hashtag. He came to stay for a weekend and we went to the football at Wembley Stadium, walked across London talking about everything. He taught me all about top surgery and as we walked up to Alexandra Palace he talked me through exactly what would happen step by step. He was the person who represented a slice of my specific dysphoria and he gave me all his knowledge. He sent me information and answered all of my questions, no matter how many or how late I sent them. Even the ones about how I would wipe my bum post-op. He shared his scars, his body, his curation with me, so that I could curate for myself.

When it came to Max, I passed that learning down. He came out to me after a queer prom night gig. With absolute honour I hugged him tight and welcomed him home. And then I told him everything Otto had told me, with my own curation packed in. I was there for the journey, offering the same solidarity and support that was gifted me. I took him to his pre-op, to his surgery, to his post-op. I got to watch him curate, and my God what a wonder it was. And later when Max meets Otto, he marvels at how Otto's scars look like mine; a matching set seems fitting.

Months later, when Seren makes that first appointment, it is Max who steps in to pass down our learning. It is Max who is sent the first reveal photos and who we FaceTime with healing questions, and it is Max who shares sibling scars with Seren. And so it always continues, our ancestry, our pain and our joy, passed on with a solidarity like nothing I have known. Together we are building something liveable.

Brighton

One weekend in February, we get the train to Brighton and River is wearing a fur coat that he found for £15. It is white and soft and like something from a fashion show and he is delighted with it. I am wearing dungarees and Freddy has a dangling skeleton earring in his right ear. We get a lot of looks; it isn't a surprise. We dance down the platform, singing and laughing. We share a double bed for the weekend. We buy the biggest jar of jalapeños and bend double with the hilarity of it. We share a bath. Our bodies normally bound and covered but not now. The gentleness of this moment, the vulnerability to see them like this, is the biggest privilege of my life. Freddy does a face mask and we are near crying with laughter when it won't come off. We cook up a feast and do tarot readings at the table. We watch a movie with popcorn and talk into the night. We triple spoon.

The morning brings coffee and seagulls and walks around junk stores. We do one of those photo booths and capture the bliss of it all in black and white. We lie on the beach and hold hands and let the wind rush around us. We run in the sea and Freddy mistimes a wave jump and gets soaked. We get tattoos, inking the words we know to be true: 'Our queer love cannot be taken, our queer joy cannot be taken.'

The sun goes down and we eat fish and chips in a tiny shop. River orders gravy on his and licks it from his fingers. We are talking about all the laws that stop us from living our lives. We are talking about marriage and adoption and love and names and then suddenly River is howling at photos of a time I tried to grow out my hair. We can't stop laughing then at his face. Tears stream down our faces and my heart is swollen with it all.

The ticket inspector lets us off when a railcard is forgotten on the way home. I make a video on my phone of the weekend while the others snooze. I am almost shocked by the utter happiness in the clips. I was not told that trans people were allowed such things. We took them anyway.

The Hospital

I worked in a London hospital for over a decade. When I first started, the smell and the white walls made my stomach churn. But slowly I got to know the way it moved, the map of all 12 floors, the wards and their people. The coffee shop would give me a free cup on the days the air was that bit heavier, the canteen ladies smiled and asked about my weekend, the stir fry guys knew my order by heart. I knew who would sub me some fresh paper when we ran short, how to fix the printer in every clinic room, the best toilets to avoid confrontation. I worked there for 11 years, grew up there, my colleagues became family. I worked on Covid wards during the global pandemic, waited for members of our team to leave ICU, cleaned my hands with floor cleaner when we ran out of soap, watched my boss cry beside a dustbin when things got really bad. I sat at the same desk for all the years I was becoming me, and I constantly taught those around me about my community. I dearly loved that hospital; I still do. It feels something like home, and yet in those 11 years there, I never did come out.

One day, leaving the hospital in a rush, I use the main toilets. While I am drying my hands as quickly as I can under the drier, an older person catches my eye.

I know what's coming, know to keep my head down. 'Was the men's closed?' she says. I pretend I can't quite hear over the sound of the air blowing over my hands and smile a sort of confused smile, hoping she will desist. She doesn't. 'Was the men's closed?' she repeats, louder this time. She doesn't know that usually I avoid this toilet, she doesn't know that I walk five minutes every time I go so that I will avoid this sort of encounter. She doesn't have any idea about any of this, about me. So I look her in the face, and smile. 'Yes, yes they were.'

It is HIV testing week, and one of the older nurses invites me to help him with testing in one of the clinics. We sit together as he talks me through the process. Another nurse comes in and asks if I am his son. There is a pause where I explain that I too work in the hospital, that I have for almost a decade. After she leaves we are quiet and I wonder if he is going to address what has just happened, if our morning together is about to become awkward. 'I have a son,' he says. It is a quiet surprise that breaks the moment, and we speak about him for a time. His life in another country, how he came to be, many things I never knew. When we fall quiet again, just before the end of the shift as we pack away the equipment, he says softly to me, 'You can be my son if you want to.'

Spring

Spring is green and pink and purple. It is sprinkling snowdrops and splashing crocuses. It is the smell of the season turning as March arrives. It is denim jackets and big boots for jumping in every puddle. It is the first glorious day you dig out your shorts and grin all day, despite the goosebumps. It is longer days and April rain macs and welly walks. It is cherry blossom and long-sleeve T-shirts. It is the approaching promise of true warmth in May. I love it.

Paper Boats

Spring tumbles into being. We still need our warm hats but the clouds are fluffier, the sun piercing through on the warmer days. It is March when Seren's grandad Iori is cremated. The day of the funeral arrives and, still in lockdown, we watch the service on a live stream. It cuts out abruptly at the end and we need to be outside. We decide to walk to the reed beds. Seren writes memories and thoughts of Iori onto a piece of paper that they then fold into a paper boat. We carry it to the reed beds where we want to put it into the river to float away. But the tide is all wrong and the riverbed is dry. We climb over a gate and into the fields where we sneak through the fence and across the mud to the closest available water. I throw stones and sticks to build a stepping-stone path across the sinking mud. When Seren reaches the water and puts the boat in, it doesn't move. Instead the paper starts to wilt. They start to cry, big, shaking sobs that crack my heart.

There is something about being trans, a sort of refusal to accept that this is all there is, that drives me. It is something that tells me to push, to believe that things can change and that I can change them. It is something that makes me explore and question and dream and make and hope. And in that moment, with the paper boat, it is the thing in me that will not accept my love standing ankle deep in mud and sobbing for a grandad whose boat won't float.

I find my way over and fish out the pink paper. I empty my pockets and find the end of a roll of microtape that has sat there since I used it to tape up my ear piercings during a football game over a year ago. I break small twigs up on the rocks and tape them together to build a tiny raft. When it is done I tape a twig in the centre, a mast, and secure the folded pink love letter to Iori on top. I carry it to Seren and they watch as I stumble to the farthest edge of the bank and push the raft into the water. We watch it float. For a moment it looks like it won't make it out of the shallows, and then it is pulled by the current downstream. We watch until it is a tiny pink speck on the horizon, and then until it is gone.

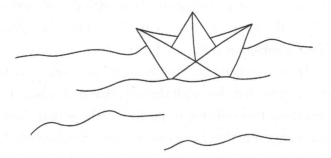

Hope is transformative. When Seren recalls the story to their mum on the phone, they both laugh bright and loud at the image of us ankle deep in mud with a soggy paper boat. Hope means that the sinking boat wasn't the whole picture, that it wasn't the end of the story. Hope means that we can laugh even when our hearts are a little broken.

Because we are always writing love letters, building makeshift rafts from scraps in our pockets, and paving the way for each other across the mud.

Observed

It is strange to be observed by others. I am read in different ways on different days by different people. I am never quite sure what makes me look one way or another. Often it happens on the Tube, people staring, trying to categorize me; I confuse them. Sometimes they discuss it out loud, as if I am not there. One day I go with Sarah to pick up Teddy from school. One of the other children points at me, 'Is that Teddy's dad?' they ask. Their mum looks up: 'That might be Sarah's brother,' she says. 'Friends,' we say, and smile all the way home.

Another day I am walking home with a takeaway pizza when four boys grab me in the street and push me up against a wall. They are shouting in my face and asking for money. All I have is my card and my pizza, which I am grabbing to my chest like a baby. 'What is wrong with you?' I manage to say. One of them comes closer into my face. I don't know what he sees, but then he is shouting and laughing, 'It isn't a boy, it isn't a boy.' There is some confusion then, some disagreement between them about what I am, and then they are running away laughing at their mistake. I walk home. There are no jalapeños in Tesco, so I start to cry. Or it might be because of the shouting, or their hands on my chest, or perhaps it is because they changed their minds and left.

One morning I wake up to my horoscope from the Co-Star app: 'Maybe someday you will know the freedom that comes with being two genders,' it says. Later, me and a friend go outside to play football on the estate. Two small kids ask to join us. 'Are you a boy or girl?' one of them asks me. 'Not really,' I say.

'Well, you're very good at football,' they reply.

A few weeks later I am nannying and I take one of the kids to play football in the park. There are about

20 primary school–aged children, and me. We are being split into teams by a 9-year-old. He looks up at me and points. 'We'll take big man,' he says. I don't think I've ever felt more powerful.

When I share a picture of me online for work, I receive hundreds of comments in reply. Comments that inform me that I am mentally ill, that I do not deserve to be resuscitated, that I will never be a boy, that I will never be a girl. I read through every comment, mildly fascinated by them all. A number of the commenters want me dead, others just think I am too unwell to have a job. They are sure they observe me, making comments about what my genitalia must be, about my state of mind, about my work. They observe me, yet they do not see me. They don't know that I love a tiny kid called Teddy with all my heart, that he calls me a boy and that brings me joy. They do not know that I love pizza and jalapeños, or that two kids in Kilburn think I'm great at football. They don't know that I nanny and that on that first hot spring day, when I used all my pay to buy us all ice cream, a 9-year-old called me big man and changed my life.

They do not see any of it.

Sam

In 2019, in March, Sam Smith comes out as non-binary; their face is all over the news. It is important because it starts conversations in the office. This is someone that people know and respect sharing a story of transness. I walk around with a glow in my chest, I'm that little bit less alone in this world, and their existence somehow validates my own.

A few weeks later, on a cold Tuesday after a long shift, I leave work and look up to see them walking up the road in front of me like some sort of magic. I run over and say thank you for their openness, their courage. 'What is your name?' they ask softly, as if it is the most important question in the world. 'Tash,' I say.

'It is so lovely to meet you Tash, I'm Sam.'

They say it as if they aren't a star, as if I don't know their name, as if they are just like me.

Two years later, in a café, with a mask over my face, the cashier asks for my name.

'Tash,' I say.

The cashier looks up. 'Sam?' they ask.

I smile and nod.

Lockdown

It is March 2020 when Covid changes everything. I call Seren and tell them that things are serious at the hospital, that things in the city might be closing soon, that we may not be able to see each other for weeks. Their voice is anxious on the phone as they tell me they are packing a bag. We have only been dating for two months, but they call me from the Tube station anyway: 'I'm on my way.' They turn up to mine with just a small bag; they've forgotten all their pants and socks. We hold each other close and I tell them it doesn't matter, I have plenty. Two years on, and all our drawers are shared. They never left.

The day lockdown is called we make a WhatsApp group and call ourselves 'Queers Against Corona', or QAC for short. We have been living in systems of mutual aid for so long that it comes naturally for us. We talk about who will stay where, making sure people won't be alone as much as we can. The first messages are about supplies and spaces to stay and stocked cupboards. But then, when we know everyone is safe, the next message, the next thing that is thought of, is art. 'If anyone wants to share art/writing/creative stuff they are doing on here, I would love to see.' After that, the chat becomes full of drawings, poems about protest and lovers, the half-formed bodies of crocheted animals. It is so typically trans: to be threatened with fear, with apocalyptic panic, and to turn to sharing art with one another.

We watch films together over FaceTime. We talk. Flori speaks about witches and writes poetry that makes my eyes burn. We send each other photos of lockdown baking – bread and cupcakes iced with trans colours. One of my favourite things is when we send photos of our morning cups of tea, it makes me feel as if we are all doing something together, it is what keeps me going through the months working on a Covid ward.

QAC becomes a family. Xan, the only one of us with a car in London, drives from house to house one day. A QAC crawl to see us all. They bring homemade potato salad with homegrown vegetables in. We sit and eat together on the grass at a distance. They throw a package to us with cookies sent from River's house. We throw back some fresh challah that they eat with a dip someone else has sent. It is like some sort of communion meal, stretched across the city, a gift.

Spring means Seren's birthday. We can't go out because the world is shut. I ask them what they would want to do if we could do anything. They would like to go to an art gallery, and then for a hike and finally to camp out for the night. So we do. I message our friends and ask them for art. Across the country our loved ones sit down to create. The next two weeks our post is filled with parcels of secret artwork. I put it all up on the walls with small descriptions like a real gallery. People have sent paintings and drawings and poems and collages. When Seren wakes up I take them into their own personal 'queerantine' exhibition. There are paintings of mountains and the stars, still lifes of fruit bowls, poems about queer kinship and about coming out, and Gabs has sent 50 photos of themself making different faces.

Seren's eyes fill with wonder, and so do mine. Because, again, when everything threatens to overwhelm us all, our friends have sent enough art to fill the walls.

Later we hike; I print screenshots of Google Maps and tape them together to make a giant map that we fold up and use to navigate us to Hampstead Heath where we eat Hula Hoops and strawberries in the sun. In the evening I make a den in the dining room with duvets and blankets, hanging fairy lights around the top. We snuggle in and fall asleep wrapped into each other. We don't take the art down for weeks, and every time I pass the room I am reminded of the creativity and glorious love of our community.

There is something about a life-altering pandemic that makes you afraid, that makes you brave. So on the last day of March, Trans Day of Visibility, I come out on social media. When I came out the first time, to myself, I never imagined I would be open in this way. When I got top surgery, I told myself that my chest would be hidden and seen only by a select few. But there is something contagious about bravery, like a row of dominoes. Pushing the first one is the start; the rest usually topple on their own.

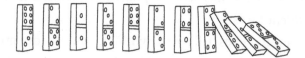

That Trans Day of Visibility I shared a little piece more of myself. One year later, to the day, I sign a book contract to write this book about trans joy. Today you are holding that trans joy in your hand, reading it and becoming part of it too.

Traditions

tradition   Passing beliefs or customs across time
              and generations.

At Easter, still in lockdown, a new QAC tradition is started: Secret Easter Bunny. We all put our names in and are each allocated a secret person to receive an Easter box. We all open them over FaceTime. There are drawings and poems and art, and chocolate of course. I receive an extra gift, a small crocheted heart. It is soft and stitched in the three colours of the trans flag. It fits in the palm of my hand and I often pick it up to hold, to remember the love that surrounds me.

We continue the Secret Easter Bunny tradition the next year. We continue the tradition of sending art, and photos of our latest baking endeavours, and Zoom calls, and games, and asking for support, and advocating for one another. It is all tradition of a sort. We didn't know a generation before us to pass down their customs and beliefs, so we make our own.

They become an amalgamation of traditions. When I come home from a bad day at the hospital, feeling like I can't be inside my body, I go outside. I take off my shoes and lie in the damp grass, looking up at the stars.

It is something I have done since I was young, but now Seren joins me and lies next to me quietly. When the water has soaked into our clothes, and the dark sky fills my eyes, I feel better.

We order a stick-and-poke tattoo set and I ink three stars onto Seren's foot. Later it is a tiny trans symbol on River's ankle. A bit after that, Seren asks me for a word on their leg. Again it is part of a tradition, a small thing that makes such a difference on the days where who we are is threatened. Something we have said to each other from the start: 'I see you.'

When they ask, Seren describes how important it has been to them, to hear it again and again and be folded into our community. My heart aches with it as I take out the needle and carefully poke the four letters into their skin: SEEN.

Happy Books

In 2012, inspired by a friend, I started a 'happy book'. A happy book is a small notebook in which every day I write three things that make me happy. I do it every night before bed religiously. It is a practice in joy documentation. The rule is that each day I write three things that made me happy that day; no matter how small they are, they go in. The only rule is that I have to find at least three things. There can be more, but there must be at least three. When I started the practice, I was deeply unhappy. Some days my three things included things like managing to shower, or sleeping through the night. Many days I struggled with making it to three things. Today I look back and read over some of the tiny moments, and some of the world-changing moments, that have brought me joy:

- rainy walks

- Fred came over and we ate pizza in the garden

- Seren sleep talking 'Love will always win'

- cycle ride in thick mud with One and Boges and Mish and picnic lunches on the canal

- Xan sent us trans love workbooks

- camping on the beach in Cornwall with Anna and La and making eggs in the morning as the sun rose

- saw a tiny hedgehog run across the road

- waking up at 4 a.m. to get the train home from

London after a gig and finding little packed break-fasts in the fridge from my aunt

- La and Anna playing games with us over Zoom

- Seren made me a birthday treasure hunt around North London and someone in the New River Café laughed at me for fishing my next clue out from a brick next to their table. When we got to the last clue, it was our bench, and Seren had written on the metal in Sharpie, 'Tash and Seren fell in love on this bench. They will come back when they are old'

- doing a protection spell for all our trans pals

- my best friend Adam's bone marrow started working after his transplant and I drank chocolate milk to celebrate

- the moment I showed Heather my new chest and she burst into tears in the kitchen

- creeping out for a walk at 3 a.m. during lockdown and the whole of the London sky was yellow

- ringing up Anna and La to ask their blessing to marry Seren. La bagsying doing the ordaining

- proposing on our bench and the writing still being

there. Sending a picture of the ring to Max and him messaging, 'I MUST CALL YOU. I'M IN ASDA'

- Adam sending me a kilogram of rainbow laces to cheer me up

- a tiny child who said very loudly, 'Is that a boy or a girl,' and I smiled so hard that they waved at me.

I read them all back and I am glad for writing them all down. It isn't often we document the joys in our life. I love that I have a decade's worth of moments kept alive in a box full of notebooks. I am glad for today, where thinking of three things comes so easily most days.

HAPPY BOOK GUIDE

1. BUY YOURSELF A LITTLE NOTEBOOK THAT YOU LOVE, AROUND A6 SIZE.

2. BEFORE BED, WRITE THE DATE IN YOUR BOOK + LIST

AT LEAST 3 THINGS THAT MADE YOU HAPPY THAT DAY.

SOME DAYS IT WILL FEEL HARD TO THINK OF 3 THINGS,

OTHER DAYS IT WILL BE EASY.

3. REPEAT DAILY.

10/04/19
· TEA + TOAST IN BED.
· CROSSWORDS WITH ONE.
· FINISHED MY BOOK.
· WALK IN THE PARK +
PHONECALL WITH LA.
11/04/19
· SPICY LENTIL SOUP AT
WORK.
· CUTE MESSAGES FROM

AD + G ♡
· FOOTBALL - SCORED
A HAT-TRICK.
12/04/19

Cai

On 8 May 2020, it is 20 years since Seren's brother died of cancer. We go for a walk through the Kilburn streets in the dark. When we leave our block of flats, I gasp. The moon is so big and so round and swollen, it floats low in the sky between the trees, a beacon, a memory. 'I was the stars and he was the moon,' Seren whispers.

We walk along the railway tracks and stand on the bridge staring at the glowing orb. Seren starts to cry. I fish two tealights out of my pocket and light them, leaving them on the railing. With our keys, I scratch Cai's name into the metal; it feels important to mark it there somehow. Seren clutches at the neck of my jacket and I fold them inside. We stand like that for a while.

I struggle to explain how courageous Seren is. They have bravery beyond anything I have known. This night when they face this yawning grief they do not shy from it, they do not turn away. Instead they watch the moon, and then the twinkling lights of the candle flames until we turn the corner. The agony of loss has not stopped them loving; it has not made them bitter or afraid to be open. They love in a way that is terrifying, so generous and whole-hearted that it burns in the corners of my eyes when I feel it.

When we get home, we play soft music and I pick up the needle and ink again. Again, they don't wince at the pain or turn from it; they breathe with the movement and at that moment I think they might be the most magnificent being in the universe.

When the clock turns midnight, I have finished inking a small crescent moon onto Seren's bicep.

Wild Swimming

When we move out of London, there is no longer a special trans swimming session. Instead there is a river and a seal that lives in it. We watch out for him every day, and on the special days he bobs up to say hello. We walk to the river at dawn. There is still frost on the ground and the river steams. We strip down and dip our toes in the icy water. I have always loved wild swimming, the battle against your own discomfort, the wonderful feeling that creeps through your bones when you beat it. When you enter ice-cold water, your body reacts with a cold shock response. The blood vessels in your skin constrict, your heart beats faster, your blood pressure goes up. The stress hormone cortisol is released, which activates the fight-or-flight response telling you to get out of the water as quickly as you can. Many athletes and wild swimmers train their bodies to calm the response. When your body is reacting with discomfort and fear at the freezing water, you must do the opposite. You must breathe slowly, relax into it, and then your body will settle. Every time you jump into that icy water, you must defeat the safety mechanisms that protect your body in order to feel the glory of the swim.

As we swim one morning, I am telling Seren about this, about the way our bodies try to protect us. They turn to me, breath steaming from their mouth and eyelashes damp with water, exquisitely beautiful. So much of our lives is spent overcoming those protections, defeating that primal need to run. So much of being trans is being faced with a fight-or-flight response, the reality of danger when leaving the house, when being who we are. Those safety mechanisms tell us to hide ourselves, to be small, to fit into the boxes we have been given. But being trans is overcoming that fear of the cold, it is breathing slowly through the cold-water shock, and it is the magnificence of our bodies sliding through the water as the sun breaks over the surface, glistening.

One day we walk along the river and there is a dog at the edge. He is whining for his ball, which is bobbing at the other side of the water. The owners are trying to pull him away, but the dog won't leave his ball. I offer to jump in and fetch it, and I take off my shoes and socks. Those safety mechanisms kick in telling me that I should hide my chest, hide myself. But I pull off my shirt and push through the water to the ball. And just as I reach it and grab it, I hear the owners from the bank: 'He is a strong swimmer. Much braver than the dog.' The dog barks joyfully at being reunited with his ball, and the owners thank me profusely. I just lie back in the water and bask in it.

Sunset

It is 5 p.m. and we are sitting in bed when suddenly we think of the sea. 'If we leave right now, we could make it for sunset.' The look on Seren's face has me jumping from the warmth of our duvet. We bundle blankets and hot water bottles into the car and head off. The golden light beams across the dashboard. I'm nervous we won't make it, but they keep saying it will be lovely anyway. They're right of course.

We scramble up the cliff slopes and find a bench in the perfect spot. The sun is a pink orb about a centimetre above the horizon; its light reflects on the underside of the clouds, turning them orange and purple. The sky is a pastel marvel. I wrap a blanket around our legs and Seren pours tea from a flask. We eat rich teas and ginger nuts as a new layer passes over the sun, turning it red like a glowing ember. It is slowly sinking onto the sea. It looks like it is melting into it. Seren tells me about being in the Lofoten islands in Norway. About how there the sunrise and sunset are sometimes so close you can watch them both in the time we have been sitting on this bench. 'You watch the sun sink into the sea, and then moments later it starts to come back up again.' I wonder what we could do with days that never end.

Summer

Summer is yellow and sky blue and ice-lolly red. It is evenings outside with chirping crickets and sand in your toes. It is T-shirts and flip-flops. It is June in the park and the buzz of life. It is July and gardens and sun loungers and sprinklers and squealing children. It is the sound of the ice cream van and the smell of barbeque. It is swimming clothes hung dripping on patio chairs. It is August in the ocean, sun cream stains and big snuggly towels. It is cycle rides and laughter and sweat and hope. I love it.

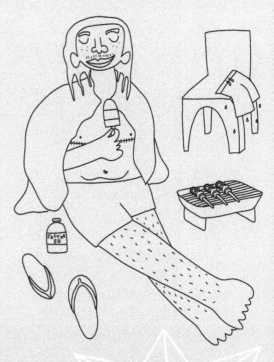

Clothes

When I was seven, I had a few items of clothes that I wore constantly. Now I am 27, it's the same. The trusted favourites that I always turn to when in doubt. I think that now I look back, it was clothes that provided my first experience of gender dysphoria and euphoria.

When I was seven, my mum loved buying me clothes I would never wear. She filled my wardrobe with tiny sailor dresses and ribbon-trimmed straw hats. The shoes with bows, and all of the frills and lace and itchy bits that made my skin crawl. I hated it all. I remember the few clothes that sat in my drawers that I adored. The white T-shirt with the phrase 'parents should be seen and not heard', the yellow hoodie with alien horns, the Thomas the Tank Engine pyjamas, which I frequently wore outside the house.

I remember shoes too. I remember standing in Clarks shoe shop having my feet measured. The lady took me over to the girls' section. The rage at the time was flashing trainers and I was desperate for a pair. Every single choice in front of me flashed pink. White with pink hearts, Care Bears and countless Bratz dolls options. I looked wistfully at the rockets, the superheroes and all the choices that filled the boys' shelves. I walked out with a pair of Pokémon trainers that day.

I remember a lot of my clothes in this way. The first pair of jeans my mother let me buy. I still remember seeing them in Tesco and that they were 12 quid. They had some sequins and beading that I didn't appreciate, but they were denim and they fit just fine. I remember the exact moment my mother finally relented to their purchase, down to the lights in the store and how my fingers trembled with the win. The excitement to watch the cashier fold them and remove the tags as she put them into a bag. Then later in the car, peeping in to check they were still there, that it was all real.

I remember the bag of hand-me-downs from the twins who lived across the road. The small black crop top and the soft leopard-print trousers that came like a gift from an angel. I adored them. The soft slightly shiny black material that lay over my flat chest and revealed my small pink tummy. The glorious velvet of the trousers and the way the ensemble seemed even more perfect together.

Clothes were an utter misery, but also a freedom and a joy. Something I realize now is, in part, connected to my transness. After years of practice, I like to boast that I can finally scout out the best cut of jeans for the transmascs. (My friends will attest to this.) I love my clothes now. My oversized hoodies, my torn jeans, my charity shop grandad jumpers, my beach shorts and 'boys' section' T-shirts, my dungarees, my colourful socks. It took me 20 years to find my own style, and my wardrobe is now formed of pieces claimed from charity shops, gifts from friends with an eye for what I would love, T-shirts hand embroidered by some especially talented pals and clothes borrowed and never returned.

As a kid I watched the girls I was friends with share wardrobes and hype each other up while they tried on each other's clothes. I always wanted that. But when it was my turn, I was the 'makeover case'. Unlike the others, I was considered unable to contribute to the process; instead I was dressed, plucked and painted under the watchful eye of a group of girls. Looking back, it was obvious then that I didn't fit, that they knew it too.

Today I have my time. We cut our hair bare-chested in the kitchen and everyone gathers round to help in the process. Except this time I am not a spectacle; I am a part of it. We bubble with nervous excitement, hair falling to the floor. And when the last cuts are made to perfection, the clippers are handed to me to exchange the favour. That trust, that companionship and mutual respect, is what I longed for all those years ago, and now it is mine.

It is mine because now I am surrounded by queerness and transness and a willingness to bend and burn down the rigidity of structures constricting my freedom. It feels like stamping on all those expectations with my kid-sized Pokémon trainers and finally wearing my truth on the outside. At least most of the time.

There is a boy I meet at uni who is from a small town in Germany. We are drawn to each other on the first day and our shared queerness spills out of us after one conversation. A few weeks into term I tell him I like his jumper. He barely hesitates before he pulls it over his head and hands it to me. 'It's yours,' he says. It is one of my favourite ever moments, so deliciously unexpected and full of love. Whenever I wear it, I think of him.

I have a lot of jumpers. They were mostly purchased a few sizes too big; sleeves trailing over my hands, I wanted them to drown me. I wanted to hide inside the folds of fabric, pull the cuffs over my hands and tie the hood strings tight until my skin was hidden within. I didn't even want to be seen, before.

Coming out and having surgery was a revolution, an injection of colour into my wardrobe. Rainbow dungarees, floral shorts, orange trainers. While my chest stitched itself back together, I discovered clothes again. Without the restrictions of a binder, I relearned the feeling of T-shirt fabric on my back, on my chest. As my nerves reached out to each other under the scars, I marvelled at the smoothness of me. I wanted to look at the angles of me, see myself in my favourite shirts again. I smiled at myself in mirrors instead of avoiding them; I actually turned towards my reflection and said, 'You look *great*.' I bought a blue polo shirt and took a photo of the wide smile on my face. This year I watched Seren re-create the same shot, in the same shirt, with the same ear-splitting grin. I turn the collar down gently and hold on while the joy creeps through us both.

There are a pair of surgery socks that are passed on too. They travel to Florida with me, hold my calves in place for weeks, then they spend two years in a drawer before Seren's turn. Our friends chip in for a surgery pillow and it is Seren's support for several weeks of healing. At the six-week mark, we reach out on a trans group and a stranger turns up on our doorstep to pick it up. They don't feel like a stranger though; we talk, and as they walk away it feels like a passing on of experience. The socks go too, with a promise to pay it forward again in time. I stop in the hallway and remember how lonely I once felt, and how now it seems there are people all across this strange world that know this part of me. That share in this slice of community. I don't feel lonely any more.

My closet has changed so many times in my life, and I am sure it will again. But as I open it up this morning, it has transformed from a place of secrets and shame to a communal wardrobe littered with hand-ons from friends and euphoria-inducing moments. I am smiling.

Top Surgery

There is no right or wrong way to be trans.

Though you would be forgiven for thinking so in a world that tells you that there is. We live within a legal system that only allows a person to change their gender with two years of proof and multiple pieces of evidence to be judged by cis people. This gender must be binary, and you have to agree that you intend to continue living in this gender until your death. There is no space for certain sorts of trans people such as me. I don't want to have my ability to choose removed because I might one day make a different choice. I want fluidity, I want the option of change without the threat of punishment.

As well as the legal system, the medical system has historically implied that there is a formula for being trans, a pathway that must be followed in order to access medical care. With gatekeeping and tick boxes in medicine, transition is often seen as a timeline to be followed, deviation seen as doubt or regret, and the possibility of transness reduced to that considered acceptable through the cis gaze.

I remember when I started coming out as trans to more people. I did it at the same time as letting them know I had booked my top surgery. When I explained that I was non-binary and was experiencing debilitating dysphoria, I was asked why that meant I needed to have surgery, as if surgery was a requirement of being trans. This was unsurprising to me given the portrayal of trans people as only legitimate if they say they are after the 'full op', or when they 'pass', or when they receive legal recognition. There was relief when I explained that my desire for surgery was mine, and not a necessity to be allowed to 'become' non-binary.

Transition, in my experience, is unique, unfixed, creative, ever-changing. Some people will be affirmed by the idea that their gender will be fixed until they die, some will only feel whole when they have accessed medical transition, some will not want any medical transition at all. All of us benefit from freedom to express, to choose, to have autonomy over our bodies. And no one person's choice should stop another from making a different one.

It is June when I get top surgery. It is booked for the day of the summer solstice. My little sister, La, texts me good luck: 'You have bravery I could only wish for.' Xan picks me and Anna up at 5 a.m. to travel to the airport. The second they heard I booked it they told me they would be there to drive me; six months later and they are. They're chatting away to keep me distracted. At the drop off they hug me tightly and I know next time I see them, hugs will be different.

Me and Ans sit in the bright airport lounge. I haven't eaten properly in days, sick with nerves. Ans brings me a cardboard dish with avo toast inside. She turns to me and says, in a voice wiser than time, 'It doesn't matter what words you use to say who you are. It doesn't matter if one day they don't fit any more. You've wanted this for so long. I know you. This is the right thing. It's all just courage.'

That sureness I once searched for, that I never found, isn't required by her. Instead, she sees what I want and believes me. Something in my chest shifts at that and a calmness settles on me. The airport avo toast is surprisingly delicious.

When we touch down it's bright and hot, the air is warm and it actually smells like Florida. I want to bottle that Florida air and take it home. It is the smell of courage to me. We travel to the seafront and the blue stretches for miles. We swim right out until all I can hear is the waves, our bags just dots on the shore. I lie on my back and starfish. The waves are licking my ears and the sun is scattering stars over the ocean. My heart jumps in my chest, the last time I'll do this for a while. With a spike of nerves, I send up a little prayer to God. I'm not sure God is something I even believe in any more, but at that moment I ask anyway: that everything I feel is real, that I can trust myself, that everything will go smoothly tomorrow.

We walk up the beach barefoot and hair dripping, carrying our shoes by their laces. As we wait for a ride home, the anxiety of it all starts to return. Then, an alert arrives on my phone from the taxi app: 'Jesus is waiting for you.' The driver has arrived and it is like a sign. A laughter that is full of relief bubbles through me as we walk to meet Jesus.

There is only one sleep before the surgeon draws felt-tip outlines on my skin. He draws the shapes that will form the new planes of my chest. Strangely, for one of the first times in years, I feel completely calm. After a wait they come to collect me, injecting something cool that makes the calmness blur at the edges. They wheel me into the operating room, lights bright above me, and just before the anaesthesia pulls me under, the final words I hear are about me...

'She's slipping under...'

'He's going to look great.'

It is hilarious to me looking back that this is the last moment that I remember before waking up. The space for my body, for me, to be seen in different ways. The desire to categorize and the limitations there. Perhaps even the surgeons who worked on my chest believed that it was them and their remodelling that was what confirmed a change in me, what legitimized my gender. I wonder if when they pulled the last stitch that sealed me up they saw themselves as fixers, or creators, as the actors of my transition.

I don't know what they thought, and I don't remember waking up. But my sister tells me that when she walked in to see me in my hospital bed, I was flirting ruthlessly with the nurses.

'You're doing an amazing, brave thing,' one of them says to me.

'Not everyone thinks so,' I reply.

'It is your life,' she says.

I don't know what the surgeons think. But when that nurse looks me in the eye and tells me it is my life, I know that she knows.

I know that she knows that this was all me, that those surgeons were just the limbs that made plain what had always been for me, that the choice was my life.

It is my life.

Recovery

Surgery for me was always about treating my dysphoria. It was about reducing the acute distress and discomfort that my chest brought me. I never realized the extent of the dysphoria until it was no longer consuming me.

Waking up in a hospital bed 4,408 miles from home, I tell Anna that I think I might have been hit by a bus, and then I smile widely. It isn't just the flatness, the lightness, the way I feel I want to open my shoulders; it is more than that. The unbearable fog in my head is gone, there is so much room, so much space. 'This is the best water I have ever tasted,' I say, partly because I haven't been allowed to drink for 24 hours and someone has stuck a tube down my throat, and partly because tasting is so much bigger now.

For six days we sit in an Airbnb and I recuperate. Most of it is spent watching crime dramas propped up in bed. Ans brings me glasses of Florida orange juice with ice in, which is my favourite thing while recovering. After two days, I take a short walk around the block in the heavy heat. Everything aches and I can't move much, but the dysphoria, that constant occupation in my head, is quiet. After six days I return to the surgeon's office to be unwrapped by the surgeon. I'm bloated and bandage marks indent my skin; there are two drains stitched into my sides that have collected blood during the week. I haven't showered since the operation and there is tape gum sticking on my chest and shoulders. When he peels the bandages away from my skin, and pulls the drain tubes out, I keep my eyes shut. Then he tells me I can look. My skin is wrinkled on my chest, but I am flat. The change for me is instant. My body seems to let out a breath it has been holding for years. I touch it gently; we don't know each other yet. There are places under my skin, ribs and muscles that I haven't felt since my teens. Nerves that are now sewing themselves back together. It feels tender right now, so I stroke my fingers across just once and then look instead. Already I am treating this body with a respect I often couldn't muster before today. Everything went smoothly, I could trust myself, and everything I felt was real. The smile cracks across my face, uncontainable.

On the car ride home, the driver thinks my bandages are because I've had a boob job like his girlfriend. I don't correct him.

The days after surgery are slow and sore. When we finally make it back to the ocean I walk along the sand, sweat forming beneath my bandages. As I walk, toes pushing into wet sand, I pick up shells. A green butterfly flits around my head. Two weeks later at home I thread the shells onto a string that now hangs in my house, a reminder of my courage and Dania Beach in Florida where I began learning to move through the world with an open chest.

When we return to the UK, I stay with my aunt Kate in Devon. Max sends me a recovery package with my first tank top in. He FaceTimes me and says, 'You look even more like you, if that makes sense.' I feel more me. It is as if I have coloured right to the edge of the lines of me, and then coloured right out. My lungs take in more air, my head tilts up, my eyes notice things that they didn't before. I am taking in everything that is still here, still beautiful and so full of life! I finally feel a part of it.

One day while walking by the river I notice a tiny dormouse in the reeds. It clings to the top of a plant, twitching its whiskers. I crouch nearby and marvel; I am full of newness. Newness like a child that makes my eyes wide and chest full. Newness that makes me want to message everyone I know and tell them how incredible they are.

I spend as much time outdoors as I can. The euphoria of having had such courage makes me giddy. I slowly get to know how to hold myself; my aunt invites her friend JQ over to teach me to stand again now my chest is open. JQ unfurls my muscles until I stand straighter. Kate tells me I have grown two inches taller, and when I stand against the tape measure it's true. JQ is 60 and at first I worry there will be a gap in understanding, but we talk and share and I come away more open, more sure.

Years later, I return to that river with Seren. We bump into JQ and they have now come out. They have tears in their eyes as they tell me how important it was to meet me those years back in my newness. We talk about family and forgiveness and growth and change and surgery. They say that we give them so much hope, we say that they give us so much hope. We tell them that it is never too late to be who you are, but really, it is them telling us that.

Sickness and Sunflowers

When the Covid-19 pandemic hit, mutual aid networks popped up all over the world. People began to organize, to remember how to live in community and support one another. For my community, and many other oppressed communities, this was not new. We were already surviving through mutual aid. So then it was us leading, teaching, passing on our wisdom. Trans people have so much to teach, about how to build safety networks, about how to redistribute, about how to care for people.

In June, the first June of the pandemic, when I have been working on Covid in the hospital for five months, we get sick. At first it is the cough and fever and so we isolate. Grace sends Freddy money so that he can pick up a shop of supplies for us. Then Xan drives the package to us. They leave it on our doorstep with a small crocheted hedgehog. When I start struggling to breathe, Xan is on the end of the phone giving Seren advice. The two of us watch crime dramas on the sofa and sleep whenever we can. Some days it is hard to walk from the bedroom to the kitchen to make food. When it gets really bad, Seren begs me to go to the hospital. I am scared. Scared of the fact that I am clearly seriously ill, but more scared of the hospital and being outed and transphobia. I don't want to go there and be alone. I think about all the times that I have sat in a waiting room with a friend, advocated on their behalf, made that phone call or pushed for better care. It has become how we do things, and I am too afraid to go alone. Seren holds my hand through the night, counting my breaths anxiously, and in the morning I can breathe a little easier. Some days I feel like I am bigger than the transphobia, that I can resist. Other days I realize that I am so afraid of the enormity of it that I cannot breathe.

On those days I cling to my community and my friends with all I can.

When we are better, Freddy, River and Xan come over. I want to reach out and touch them, hold them. Instead we go for a distanced walk in the rain. Fred finds a mug on the street and takes it home. We sit outside and drink tea. River and Fred have got us sunflowers, bright yellow and alive. Sunflowers are my favourites. When they are growing, their heads turn throughout the day as they follow the sun across the sky, seeking out the light and warmth. They also are incredible absorbers of toxins and have been used to clean the soil after radiation contamination in Fukushima and Chernobyl. They are made up of thousands of smaller flowers but stand as one. I love that, the solidarity of it. They are resilient, they are healers. They follow the light, moving together as a field of golden faces. A thousand, thousand flowers, all chasing the same sun.

One weekend, me and Seren take our tiny tent and catch the train into the country. We walk with our packs through fields and over hills. It is hotter than we expect and we run out of water before our next fill point. We eat fat berries off the bushes, and I tell Seren to suck the moisture out of even the bad ones because we are so dehydrated. We are laughing but we also have no idea what we will do. Just as things start to look desperate, we round the corner and there is a field of beautiful sunflowers. We forget about the water for a minute as the golden hour light illuminates them all in perfect yellows. Watching Seren's eyes widen and their face bathed in sunset, it is the moment I know I will marry them. I take the coordinates down on my phone because I want to remember that moment, the perfectness of it.

When we finally leave the field and round the next corner, we spot a house, the first in miles. There is a huge skull and crossbones flag flying from the chimney. We debate whether our thirst is bad enough to accept the embarrassment of not packing enough water, and we eventually decide we may die if we don't drink soon. We approach the skull and crossbones house and knock on the window. Someone waves from inside. 'Help yourself to water,' they say, pointing to an outdoor tap. 'It comes from a natural well.' We drink till our bellies are full and then fill our bottles too. Afterwards we head back to those sunflowers and pitch for the night. When dawn breaks on the new day, their faces have turned to greet the sun once again.

Seaweed

The next June, when restrictions finally ease, we decide to camp. Freddy and Xan drive down from London. We meet at the campsite in Devon and when we hug, for the first time in over a year, there are fat tears in my eyes. The four of us put up the tents and the gazebo that we communally bought for lockdown meetings in the rain. It now acts as a shade maker in the glorious sunshine. Xan lights the barbeque and we cook veggie sausages and halloumi. The space is soft and the sun dips over the tree, bathing us all in golden light. We have hot chocolate and laugh and laugh and laugh. In the morning we cook vegan bacon and then walk to a café at the top of the hill. We get iced coffees and discuss the perils of public toilets. Then we head to the river and strip to our trunks on the bank. Two kids discuss our scars, whispering behind their hands. 'They all have the same marks,' one says to the other. The water is beautiful and there are tiny fish swimming by our feet. The light bounces off the surface, illuminating our faces. Three years previously, when I had imagined swimming after top surgery, I thought I would cover myself, hide the scars, pretend. But when we look back on the photos after, I stand tall, laughter caught in my face, chest open. When I look back, I am stood between my friends, and we have the same marks, and the same beaming smiles.

Lying on the bank drying out, we watch people watching us. Across from us there is a small child running about in just a T-shirt. There is a mutual understanding about that childhood freedom that the four of us share in a look. That perfect joy of a kid experiencing the grass on their bare feet. It is a moment of collective joy that we share, a sort of nostalgia but also recognition, the grass whispering against our own new bare chests. And then, loudly, shockingly, the person looking after the child farts. It is too loud and long to ignore and we try to suppress our laughter. But like children it only makes it spill out faster; hands over mouths we giggle like school kids. Big, convulsing joy, the sort that continues all day and re-erupts whenever you catch each other's eyes.

We eat what we decide are the best pies of our lives that night. As we fill our bellies, a crow descends on the next-door pitch and makes off with a whole pot of hummus. The sight of the crow, hummus in beak, is enough to free that laughter again. We are still laughing when the sun dips below the trees, bleeding the sky pink. We start telling stories. Stories of our childhoods and the moments we learned and grew, and when we met and re-met. I have known so much of these people, so many different times and versions of them. Fred turns to me. 'You are so, so important to me,' he says. 'I love you.' As the trans colours leak through the clouds, I think to myself that I love all the versions of him, from all of the times. But in this moment, this version, this Fred right now, is the one that I love the most.

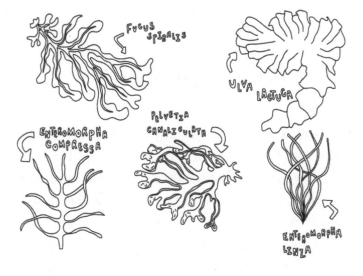

Morning starts with eggs and fresh bread. We drive to the ocean and swim in the cove. We talk about seaweed, and when I am returning to shore I remember that I have always been that bit afraid of seaweed. But today, when Fred speaks of it with a reverence in his voice, an understanding of the magic of their colours and shapes, the way they breathe with the ocean's lungs, I let their slippery fingers touch my legs. And this is how trans people change me. It is in the way they see things, the way they sit with discomfort, the way they teach about the spaces in-between. Freddy is right: the seaweed is beautiful.

A Summer to Remember

We spend a lot of time outside that summer. We rent a house with Tilly and Flora and their cat, Bug. The house has big windows and a hundred plants that hang from the ceiling and in the shower. There is a seagull who lives on the roof and greets us every day with a call that sounds like he is laughing at us. He hates when we use the toilet and glares through the skylight, beady-eyed and tapping on the glass between screams. The days are long and full of sunshine. We work in the heat with tall glasses of Flora's iced coffee and then when we clock off, we steal the last rays of gold from the evening.

We take old jam jars filled with cucumber and carrots down to the river and sit under the trees. We swim and play cards and read our books. We talk in the fading sunshine about bodies and gender and the sweetness of strawberries. We pick garlic leaves from the bank on the way home and make garlic bread. There are broccoli spears and pods of brilliant green peas from the garden. We eat pizza outside and play board games on the living room floor. One day we rescue an injured crow from the road and name her Mae. We take her to the bird-doctor who lives next door and when she dies overnight, we all cry. We drive to the sea and Tilly gets car sick on the way and vomits out of the window. We cry with laughter at the side of the car when we arrive. We share in that house – clothes, books, meals, parts of ourselves.

It is a home that is full of joy.

Tilly comes out in that house. With Flora they chalk TRANS PRIDE on the garden paving slabs. We spend one glorious summer with them, swimming and sun-kissed, toasting marshmallows on the fire, growing more ourselves. When it is time to part, Tilly says it has been a time of healing. All of that joy made us better.

We Are Everywhere:
Trans Pride Brighton

July is Trans Pride in Brighton. I get the train to the sea with Max. I am wearing rainbow dungarees and Max has crafted himself a glitter beard. People stare at us on the train, but when we arrive there are so many of us that we fill the streets. We join Otto and Arlo and Elliot and stand in the crowd. When we march it feels so powerful; people cheer from their cars. Together we wind along the seafront to the square, spilling onto the grass with picnics and smiles. There are trans parents and trans families and older trans people. The whole place is bursting with possibility and potential. It is the first time I have seen trans people in such a space, lifting their babies onto their shoulders, holding hands, faces painted; we are surrounded by trans joy. The sun is blazing and my scars are out. A woman approaches us and asks us to come and speak to her friend Jean about what the day is about. Jean is from a small village in Bedfordshire. She is 76 and walks with a frame. She smiles up at us as we talk to her. She doesn't say much but she smiles with her eyes, and before we walk away she says, 'If something makes you happy and more yourself, then you should go for it.'

We sit on the beach and walk into the sea and the whole stretch of the shoreline is filled with trans people. There are people shirtless, people with binders and T-shirts and dresses in the ocean, laughing, squealing. We are everywhere. When we walk home I realize how much of myself I usually hide, how important community is. Two years later and I am back at Brighton Beach. I swim with my friends and there is a woman watching us from the shore. When we get out she speaks to one of the group: 'It is so amazing to see somebody trans, with their scars out, swimming and so happy. My brother has just come out as trans.'

We are everywhere.

Milton Sands

Just before July slips away, we drive to Milton Sands. We wait for them by the café, kicking our feet in the sand. When they arrive, the four of us go straight to swim. Me and Seren walk down to the waves and the mum and her kid follow. We all get in, yelling at the cold of it. We can't really hold a conversation yet, so we just battle against the ocean, who keeps sweeping us up. Seren brings a hand out of the water and they are holding the husk of a watermelon slice that has been discarded in the sea, and the weirdness of it makes us all laugh. When we get out, we dry off and get hot chocolate with tiny marshmallows. We sit on a wooden bench and then we talk. This 14-year-old is one of the most grounded kids I have ever met. They are articulate and honest and they speak about their body and their gender in a way that it took me years to achieve. Their mum is asking the questions, making sure, asking for our experiences. She is afraid for her kid, but she is fierce in her love in a way that makes a mark on me so deeply. We spend hours there, eating chips and sandwiches and anything else the café offers. We talk about school and toilets and puberty and relationships. We talk about Minecraft and Doctor Who and swimming. None of us want to leave, I can feel it, like a lull in the universe. Sat here on this bench is a moment for us all.

When we finally admit that we are all freezing, we walk back to our cars. Seren hands them an envelope of artwork. I have tears in my eyes and I'm not the only one. When we wave goodbye, Seren says, 'It's so weird how you can see someone for such a short time and they feel like family.'

The mum texts me later: 'Just knowing you exist gives me hope for my kid.'

I think of them often. The power of a kid who says what they need, and a mother who listens.

Swimming and Coasters

The first August that me and Seren spend together, we travel to Wales with my family. It is the first time me and Seren have gone to the beach together. They haven't swum in years, but when me and my siblings run yelling into the sea, they are there. The joy of it is overwhelming. I give La piggybacks in the water and we are all crying with laughter at the gulls who think Anna's shaved head is something to eat. They circle above and every time one swoops down towards her, we all scream with delight.

It sounds a small thing to swim, but not for us. We eat ice cream and play cricket until the tide comes in, stranding us, and we squeal with the adventure of wading across the stream of water with all of our things. I collect tiny shells and stones and hold them in my hands, as if I can take a piece of this day home with me. I keep them and later send a small envelope of that beach debris in the post to Otto. Weeks later a parcel arrives for us. Three exquisite coasters, those shells and stones from that first ocean swim together, set perfectly in resin. Now, every time I set my tea down, I remember that day and that swim and how truly, deeply happy it felt.

I truly love that about my friends – their desire to keep tangible our joy. To preserve it and keep it present in our everyday lives. I have coasters and embroideries and walls full of artwork and poetry and notes. I have photos and letters and socks and passed-on clothes and shells and soft toys. We are like living museums of our love for one another and our community. Our protection, our preservation, lives among us.

If I Had My Time Again

August bank holiday I head to a festival; it is my first since top surgery and I am nervous. When we arrive it is so hot that everyone strips down to bikini tops and shorts. We are putting up the tents and we are all dripping with the heat. After a short debate with myself, I pull off my shirt. It feels monumental but nobody seems to notice or care. The rest of the heatwave weekend I walk around shirtless, dungaree straps over my shoulders. I bump into some friends I have not yet come out to. They see my chest, my scars, the wideness of the smile on my face. Later one of them slips me a note that says she has never seen me so happy, so free.

Fred is there and we are sitting under a tree one morning when we witness a tiny baby take their first steps. It is pure magic. I feel a bit like I too am taking first steps. I'm wobbly, but full of courage. When the sun goes down, we sit on a blanket in a big group while some of us queue for hot chocolate. I overhear some adults on the table beside us talking. They are talking about how they have seen people here who wore skirts but had beards, people who they couldn't categorize into a binary gender, people who filled them with disgust. Their faces are twisted up like they don't want to see such people again. The courage of my first steps has me standing and going over to them. 'Excuse me,' I say. 'I'd just like to chat to you because I'm one of those people you are talking about.' After that, we talk for an hour. They say that things are so different now, they can't agree, they can't understand, we are just too far apart. We talk some more and I tell them about the pain of gender, the things that hurt me. Then the one with the deepest frown lines starts to talk about school days and growing up and feeling left out and excluded. And then, suddenly, they see that we are talking about the same thing, the same harms. It is a moment I will remember for the rest of my days when they lift their head and look me in the eye. 'I think, actually, if I had my time again, I would do things your way.'

Suddenly the distance between us doesn't seem so far. Suddenly the great yawning gap that most days threatens to swallow me whole seems to reach together, and grasp hands in the middle.

Ladybirds

Three years later, we return to that same space. Yet this time it is a whole crew of us. When we arrive, Lu greets us and we build our tents together. We play cards and share food. We create a small, transient community. I met Lu on a retreat for queer people where they became my sibling overnight. We talked over cards with bright images and one with a ladybug stood out to us both, the joyfulness and sacredness of such a tiny creature. Later we walked along the coast and ate samphire that was growing in the sand. We saw a ladybird land nearby as we walked and it felt so deliberate, so important, that we looked up what ladybugs symbolize. According to the internet, the ladybug is 'an ally for graceful transitions'. After that, we message one another whenever we see a ladybug. It is our link in a busy world. Lu says it reminds them of our joy.

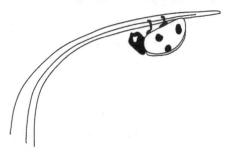

Lu introduces us to their wife, Kat. When the group becomes larger and we are all talking, I hear Kat say, 'Sorry, I missed what your pronouns are' to someone across our circle. It is said so simply, so easily, and received so welcomely that my heart warms in my chest. When we leave Lu sends me a photo of a ladybug that has landed on their hand.

I text them about it now, about writing about trans

joy, and their reply brings me to tears: 'Well, for the first time I felt trans joy when I met you.'

JQ

We meet up with JQ one weekend and sit outside drinking iced coffee. We pass on our knowledge, our stories. It feels like a craft that some have long forgotten, but storytelling is one of our powers. We speak of childhood and ageing and bodies. We speak of forgiveness and change.

Trans people do a lot of forgiving. There is a lot of patience needed in transition, a lot of grace. Forgiveness for others, for those we lose, for ourselves. Transition gave me a whole new bucketful of grace for myself, and that bled into my relationships. Transition is realization, actualization of me. And that gives me the courage to want for myself, to draw boundaries, to heal age-old wounds.

When we meet again with JQ weeks later, we sit in their garden with slices of Soreen and butter. Together we apply for their surgery. They write their answers and we have the honour of being there. The form asks when they first felt discomfort with their body. They recite aloud in stilted sentences as they type: 'For 50 years, but especially since puberty cast its long, dark shadow over my life.'

Fifty years of shadows seem to clear from their face as they submit the form. They stand, as if too excited to stay seated, and wipe a tear from behind their glasses. They squeal. It is a sound of delight, promise, forgiveness, and I wonder about the courage of 50 years, half a century. The courage of hope held for more than 18,000 days. A feat I almost couldn't imagine, except it is written all over their face.

Impossible

When I first realized I was queer, lots of the things I thought my future would hold no longer seemed possible. For a long time, having a future at all was in question. One of the biggest things that was lost was the image of having a family of my own. When I came out as trans, that picture slipped a little further away, and after top surgery further still. I couldn't fit myself in the image because I couldn't imagine it. I didn't think that possibility was for me any more, and so, I let it go.

When I see a trans parent carry a child for the first time, my heart stirs. Years later when my friend Jay sends photos of their one-year-old, I start to wonder. When I meet trans papas and families with non-binary parents it moves me. I follow families from all over the world on social media, watching them raise their children in vibrant ways, in new ways, in the ways of their ancestors, in completely remarkable and completely unremarkable ways. It changes me.

It is 3 a.m. and we can't sleep. We are chatting into the dark about the things that bumble around your head in the early hours. There is a stillness in the air. We are talking about possibility. I am telling Seren about the trans parents I know who have been able to body feed their babies after surgery, about how despite their chests being completely restructured and their nipples regrafted, their bodies have created new pathways to allow the milk through. This was something we were told was impossible. And then we are talking about all the things that have been impossible for trans people. And about how perhaps those impossible things never really were impossible. That in fact, just by simply existing, we create possibility for one another.

They said we couldn't have children, but I have seen them. They said we would never have peace, but I have seen it. They said joy wasn't something our lives would know, but I have felt it. They said no so many times that we stopped asking permission and just tried instead, our literal bodies becoming sites of resistance, of creation, of hope.

When we finally close our eyes again, my head is filled with new pictures. Pictures that hold tiny hands and feet that don't yet exist, but that I now know can be possible.

Possible

We dream of a big house; we call it 'the commune'. It has plants and herbs in window boxes, and rows of sunflowers in the garden. There are butterflies and bees and a vegetable garden. Inside there is art on every wall, big prints and paintings and even scribbles from tiny hands learning to make colours and shapes. There is space for everyone and yet there is still always some-one crashing on the sofa with a huge blanket, finding a place to call home. There is music of course, singing and guitars and composing the harmonies of a shared life. There are so many books from every genre; a stack in the bathroom has poetry, fantasy, crochet patterns, textbooks, sheet music. Clothes hang on the line together, and someone is baking in the kitchen and the smell drifts through the air.

In the commune there is space for fear and sadness and grief too. We hold it gently in the palms of our hands and then we set it down together to accept a warm brew. The mug collection in the kitchen is obviously incomparable. We have conversations in snippets as we buzz about our lives, and then all at once over a big meal in the evening. There is always someone up late so you are never alone when you walk downstairs to fetch a hot water bottle in the early hours.

We share the burdens of life in this world. We string the Samhain fairy lights across the roof, and under them we dance. We twirl together, chests open and eyes bright, out of breath with happiness. We share clementines and make big cauldrons of stew. We go to the beach and we swim. There are piles of shells and rocks littered on the shelves, memories of so many good days. Photos hung with tiny pegs on strings that stretch from one wall to another.

Like now, we are each other's insurance systems. We

share. We give back. We teach each other the things we know. About how to forage for the best mushrooms, about how to write a song, about how to care for yourself after surgery. There are clothes in the drawers that belong to everyone here, and socks that belong to nobody.

We paint the walls ourselves. A mural in every room, stories of the vibrancy of our joy. Everyone has their bit of the space. A room filled with a thousand houseplants, a room with guitars hung from the ceiling, a room just full of books. We find most of the furniture in charity shops or left in the street for rehousing. And we do what we always do, we carry it home and we sand it down and we paint it until it is something new, like us.

In the commune there are traditions. We always have a dance party when we wash up. If you make a tea, you make one for everyone. Storytelling is sacred. There are so many ways of saying I love you and we use them all. 'I'll pick up milk on my way home', 'Don't forget to take your meds', 'I watered your plants for you', 'Do you need a hand?'

There is still anger and there is still pain. It wouldn't be real if there wasn't. There are still days when it feels impossible to get out of bed, days when the crushing weight of illness and anxiety and bills feels too much.

We know those days only too well. When they happen, we don't hide them any more. We sit together in the quiet of it. Sometimes there is crying, sometimes there is holding, sometimes there is a long walk in the crisp air to fetch coffee and doughnuts. Sometimes there is planning and spreadsheets, phone calls to phone companies to get the bills down. Sometimes there is recycling and reusing and asking for help. Sometimes there is painting banners and placards and shouting in the streets until our feet hurt and our throats are sore. Sometimes it is a movie together, popcorn and an early night. Sometimes it is serious chats and someone to come with you to the doctor. Sometimes it is waiting patiently until the sky clears, and sometimes it is putting on wellies and raincoats and jumping in every single puddle as the heavens open. The commune weathers it all.

It is a dream, but like so many things now, it feels possible.

Ma

My grandma Ma is the one who first wrote with me. We wrote poems together and she always told me that they were fantastic, always encouraged me to write, to create. One day recently we visit her and she pulls out photos and old school reports in that way grandparents do. She asks who the handsome man I have brought with me is, and Seren beams. Then she digs out a book and in it is a poem she wrote for me many years ago. It is dated 8 February 2006 and dedicated 'To my 12-year-old grandchild'.

There is so much you seem to know about life
Twelve years only you have lived –
But I can see the change in your eyes
As you look ahead.

How do you know what the world will be like?
As you stand at the threshold.
You seem to know you will have to make choices
Learn to suffer and enjoy.
Does your brain prepare you for this
As your body grows?

You seem to know about people, injustice, beauty –

As your own beauty changes into maturity.
It is as if all the things you learnt are being
Slowly released to prepare you for your future –

To give a wisdom you are beginning to seek.
I can see the change in your eyes
There is so much you seem to know about life.
Yet, you are still a child.

The poem is entitled 'The Transition'.

Samhain Again

The years pass. It is Samhain again and this time we print photos of our loved ones lost. We display them in frames on a makeshift altar. We sit with cups of tea and bowls of hot stew and we speak about those who are in the photos. We tell stories, share memories of them, honour them. We laugh about the time my grandma J got a caution for running my grandad over in Sainsbury's car park after offering to back the car out of a small parking space with no driving licence.

We write the things we want to let go of on pieces of paper and burn them in the flames. Then we speak aloud the things we are grateful for: each other, being outside, being brave, support of our community, healthcare, relationships, trans joy. Then Fred throws some burning incense in the flames and the smell washes around us. We are standing around the fire now and we hold hands for a moment that feels so easy and powerful. It is our own magic.

Trans joy is so often forgotten. It exists despite systems that seek to destroy us. It exists in the relationships we have and in our courage to be and create. It is in the seaweed and the sunflower fields, it is in the roll of the ocean and the setting of the sun, it is in dancing and chosen family and mutual aid and community healthcare. It is the turn of the seasons, always driving, always pushing things to grow and change, always gloriously, achingly beautiful. Always on its way, across and beyond.

Trans joy exists because we exist.

Trans joy is resistance.

I wrote this book because I never got to read it when I was 15, or 18, or 25. I wrote it for all the versions of me that needed it. I wrote it for every trans person who is waiting for the world to change.

I wrote it for you too. I hope it brought you joy.

(Mile)stones

I have a bowl of stones in my room. Each stone is labelled in Sharpie with where and when I got it. I pick them up when I have one of those moments – the type where you feel something inside you aligning, the type you want to hold on to and bottle up in a mason jar. When those moments happen, I pick up a stone. I carry it home in my pocket and then it goes in the bowl. There are about 30 stones in there now. The first time I swam in the sea topless, a moment I achieved some peace, a weekend trip to Brighton with friends, Trans Pride, the day I knew I wanted to marry my partner, the first time we swam *together* topless, the first time they successfully skimmed a stone. Moments that feel like milestones, like beads on the string of my life. Sometimes I sit with the bowl and I take them out one by one and hold them. I like holding the weight of those memories in my hands.

Sometimes the things that make the bowl are surprising – I have a stone from a day when we screwed up the dates on our holiday and had to clean and pack everything in under an hour. After abandoning our last day, we drove to the ocean and swam with 20-foot stormy waves under a grey sky. We were wrecked, bruised and shivering. My six-foot-tall uncle crawled out on his hands and knees, and we laughed so hard we couldn't breathe. It was one of the best moments of my life. I love that stone.

So maybe try starting a bowl and see what you keep. I like to sit down with people and share the stories of each stone – one day maybe you will share yours.

I hope your bowl gets full.

Acknowledgements

Thank you to everyone at JKP, especially for the competition that made space for writing about everyday transness. Thank you to Andrew James for believing in me, for being so sure that I could write this book and for asking enough times that I said I would.

Thank you to my Ma who taught me that I could create, and who gave me permission to share a poem of hers in this book just before she died.

I feel like so much of this book wrote itself because of the incredible people in my life. I love you all with all I am.

Finally, Flatboy, thank you for making beautiful art for me to share in these pages. Everything you do is glorious.